TIME AND TIDE

The Archaeology of the Witham Valley

Edited by Steve Catney and David Start

Proceedings of the Witham Archaeological Seminar of December 2001

Published by the Witham Valley Archaeology Research Committee

TIME AND TIDE

© Individual authors and the Witham Valley Archaeology Research Committee
First published in the United Kingdom in 2003 by
The Witham Valley Archaeology Research Committee
c/o Heritage Trust of Lincolnshire
The Old School, Cameron Street
Heckington, Sleaford
Lincolnshire NG34 9RW

British Library Cataloguing in Publication Data:
A CIP catalogue record for this book is available from the British Library
Catney, S. and Start, D. (eds)
Time and Tide The Archaeology of the Witham Valley
ISBN 0 948639 40 7

This volume is published with the aid of grants from English Heritage, the Environment Agency, the Highways and Planning Directorate of Lincolnshire County Council and the Heritage Trust of Lincolnshire.

All rights reserved. No part of this publication may be reproduced or transmitted in any form or by any means, electronic or mechanical, including photocopying, recording or any information storage and retrieval system, without permission in writing from the publisher.

Designed by Susan Unsworth
Printed in the UK by G W Belton Ltd, Gainsborough

Front cover illustration: The Witham shield – an Iron Age treasure found in the river Witham near Lincoln in 1826. It is formed of beaten bronze with a raised spine and three bosses decorated in La Tène style. ©Copyright The British Museum

Witham Valley Archaeology Research Committee

CONTENTS

List of Contents iii
List of Contributors iii
Acknowledgements iv
Foreword iv

Introduction
1. Strategy Study For The Lower Witham 1
   by Andrew Usborne
2. Setting The Scene 3
   by Steve Catney

Man In The Valley
3. 'Coming From Bardney ...' – The 6
   Landscape Context Of The Causeways
   And Finds Groups Of The Witham Valley
   by Paul Everson and David Stocker
4. The Fiskerton Causeway: Research - 16
   Past, Present And Future
   by Naomi Field, Mike Parker Pearson and Jim Rylatt

The Natural Valley
5. Palaeoenvironmental Research Design 33
   For The Witham Valley
   by Charly French and James Rackham

Managing The Valley
6. Local Authority Cultural Resource 43
   Management
   by Jim Bonnor and Steve Catney
7. Management Through Other 52
   Mechanisms
   by Dave Went

Managing The Finds From The Valley
8. Conservation Of Excavated Finds 60
   by Rob White

Involving The Community
9. Site Management And Interpretation 66
   In The Local Community
   by David Start
10. Presentation To The Wider World 76
    by Thomas Cadbury

Conclusion
11. The Archaeology Of The Witham Valley: 81
    Something *Has* To Be Done
    by Francis Pryor

CONTRIBUTORS

Jim Bonnor, Senior Built Environment Officer, Highways & Planning Directorate, Lincolnshire County Council, City Hall, Lincoln LN1 1DN

Thomas Cadbury, Keeper of Collections Management, City and County Museum, 12 Friars Lane, Lincoln LN2 5AL

Steve Catney, Conservation Services Manager, Highways & Planning Directorate, Lincolnshire County Council, City Hall, Lincoln LN1 1DN

Paul Everson, English Heritage, National Monuments Record Centre, Great Western Village, Kemble Drive, Swindon SN2 2GZ

Naomi Field, Lindsey Archaeological Services, 25 West Parade, Lincoln LN1 1NW

Charly French, Department of Archaeology, University of Cambridge, Downing Street, Cambridge CB2 3DZ

Mike Parker Pearson, Dept of Archaeology and Prehistory, University of Sheffield, Sheffield S1 4ET

Francis Pryor, Inley Drove Farm, New Fen Dyke, Sutton St James, Spalding, Lincolnshire PE12 0LX

D. James Rackham, The Environmental Archaeology Consultancy, 25 Main Street, South Rauceby, Sleaford, Lincolnshire NG34 8QG

Jim Rylatt, Senior Project Officer, Pre-Construct Archaeology (Lincoln), Unit G, William Street Business Park, Saxilby, Lincoln LN1 2LP

David Start, Heritage Trust of Lincolnshire, The Old School, Cameron Street, Heckington, Sleaford, Lincolnshire NG34 9RW

David Stocker, English Heritage, 23 Savile Row, London W1S 2ET

Andrew Usborne, Project Team Manager, The Environment Agency, Kingfisher House, Orton Way, Orton Goldhay, Peterborough PE2 5ZR

Dave Went, English Heritage, 23 Savile Row, London W1S 2ET

Rob White, Principal Keeper - Conservation, Lincolnshire County Council Heritage Service, Conservation Department, Education & Cultural Services Directorate, Lincolnshire Archives, St Rumbold Street, Lincoln LN2 5AB

Acknowledgements

Paul Everson and David Stocker wish to thank their colleagues Philip Sinton (Fig. 1), Tony Berry (Fig. 2) and Simon Crutchley (Fig. 6) for originating illustrations. They are grateful to Mike Parker Pearson and Naomi Field for discussion of their forthcoming report on excavations at Fiskerton in advance of its publication.

In addition to thanking the authors of the papers, who have all played their part splendidly, Steve Catney and David Start wish to acknowledge the contribution of the sponsors of this volume: English Heritage, The Environment Agency; Lincolnshire County Council; and The Heritage Trust of Lincolnshire. We are grateful for the support and advice of the Witham Valley Archaeology Research Committee and in particular the practical assistance of Francis Pryor in the face of dissolving deadlines. Our thanks for advice and assistance must go to Mark Bennet, Lou Burton, Sarah Grundy, Allan Hall, Doug McElvogue, Kate Mitchell and Jon Watson and for permission to use illustrations, to the British Museum, Chris Cox, Chris Cruickshank, Getmapping plc, the National Monuments Record, David Robinson and John Turner. We would like to make special mention of Susan Unsworth, who designed and typeset this volume, and David Hopkins, who carried out much of the artwork.

Foreword

Regional archaeology can sometimes be parochial in both scope and significance. In these instances its justification is that it contributes towards a bigger picture ... but the material covered in this volume is different. Yes, it is small-scale in scope and it does indeed contribute towards a developing synthesis of Fenland archaeology, but there is far more to it than that. In fact to describe the work in this book as parochial is entirely to miss the point, because it addresses themes which are both universal and profound.

Archaeology is the humanity, perhaps above all others, which can examine the development of human society over huge expanses of time. As archaeologists we are inclined to pay lip service to this diachronic, or time-depth, approach to the past, while at the same time we confine our research to the narrow time slices with which we are all personally familiar. The archaeology of the Witham valley, however, demands a different strategy: it has to be approached through time and from a number of angles. Nothing else will do. It is no use, for example, to wonder why the various Witham abbeys are so located without also thinking about the distribution of Bronze Age barrow cemeteries and Iron Age causeways. These themes must be set against the backdrop provided by a constantly changing, and frequently very wet, environment.

If temporal continuity is one major theme, ritual or religion has to be another, for few rivers in Britain can provide 'offerings' as rich and varied as the prehistoric Witham shield, the Fiskerton sword hilt or the Washingborough hanging bowl. None of these superb objects was lost by accident. So we must explain not only why they were deposited, but why they were deposited in a small, flat river valley within sight of Lincoln city. These, and other finds from the old course of the river, are superbly preserved artefacts. The waterlogged ground conditions on the valley floor also preserve excellent environmental deposits. Away from the river itself, the higher parts of the valley sides favour aerial photographs and field survey. These different, but complementary conditions allow a broader picture of settlement through time to be developed. Few areas of Britain can offer greater archaeological potential.

Research into the archaeology of the Witham valley is both a big intellectual and practical challenge, and the various contributors to this volume have risen to it with flair and imagination. I can also proclaim, thanks to the newly inspired Witham Valley Archaeology Research Committee, that much exciting new work is in active preparation. If sometimes regional studies can be only too easy to set to one side, may I suggest that you continue reading. Turn the page. You have a treat in store.

Francis Pryor
Chairman,
Witham Valley Archaeology Research Committee

STRATEGY STUDY FOR THE LOWER WITHAM

by Andrew Usborne

Strategy Study

In 1997 the Agency completed a Strategy Study for the Lower Witham system between Lincoln and Boston. The river Witham and its tributaries drain over 2000 km^2 of South Lincolnshire and there are over 300 km of raised embankments between Lincoln and Boston that need to be maintained and, where possible, improved.

There are two main problems in the area. The first is that the embankments are in a poor condition and in places they need to be raised and strengthened. The second problem is that there is insufficient capacity within the embankments during a flood event leading to excessive seepage and a significant risk of the system breaching. This will be resolved by the provision of flood storage areas.

The study showed that out of the 300km of embankments over 30 km required works within the first 5 years (Fig. 1). The works consist of raising and widening the embankments by importing clay to rebuild the back of the embankments. This increases the capacity of the river system and also significantly reduces seepage through the banks thereby reducing the risk of a catastrophic breach. There is also a need to ensure that the embankments do not fail due to erosion from the toe and to stop this limestone rock is placed at the toe (Fig. 2).

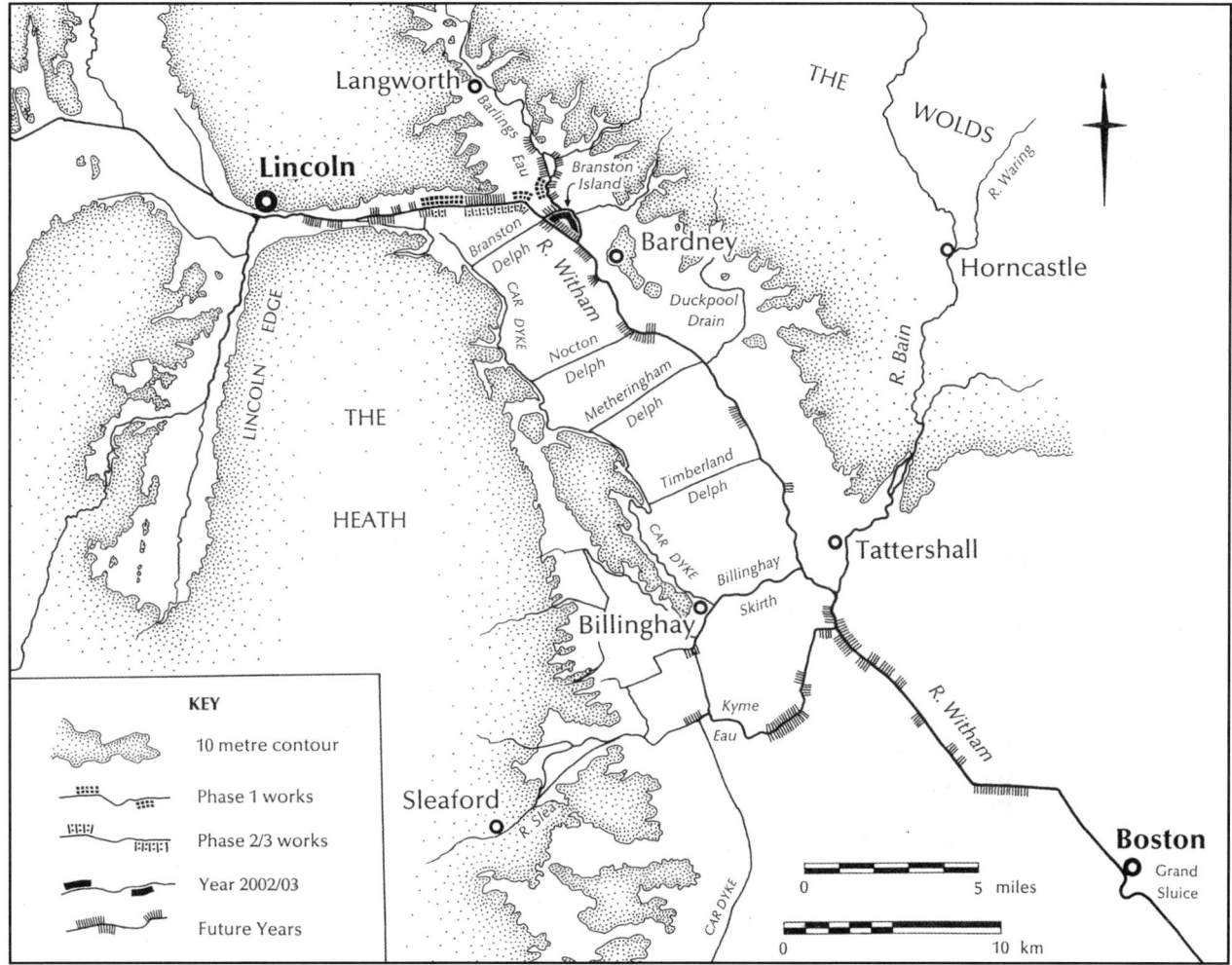

Figure 1 The lower Witham and its tributaries. Work is planned on over 30km of river embankments between 2001 (phases 1, 2 and 3) and 2006.
Drawn by D.W. Hopkins

The works to the river Witham are being delivered by an integrated team led by the Environment Agency. May Gurney Civil Engineering of Norwich are implementing the works which have been designed by Bullen Consultants of Bradford.

The provision of flood storage areas will enable excess flood water to be stored on adjacent farmland. Whether this land is turned into an environmental asset or remains being farmed is currently under discussion with the appropriate landowners.

As part of these works the Agency carried out an archaeological desk top assessment. However, once the Iron Age causeway was excavated the Agency, in conjunction with the County Archaeologist, reviewed the assessment and appointed Pre Construct Archaeology to carry out further in-depth studies focussing on the areas where the Agency were proposing to carry out construction works.

The key driver for the Environment Agency is to provide improved flood protection for the people of Lincolnshire, at the same time enhancing the environment generally as well as safeguarding the archaeological heritage. As a result of this strategy the Agency will, wherever possible, be using clay sources adjacent to the river. We have already taken over 80,000 m^3 from a new pit at Fiskerton by barge on the river to build up the embankments. The works on the river also involved the provision of fish refuges in the berms, a wetland margin to help create a stable reed bed and owl boxes to provide nesting for barn owls. At the close of the project the clay pit will be handed over to Lincolnshire Wildlife Trust to be managed as a wetland reserve.

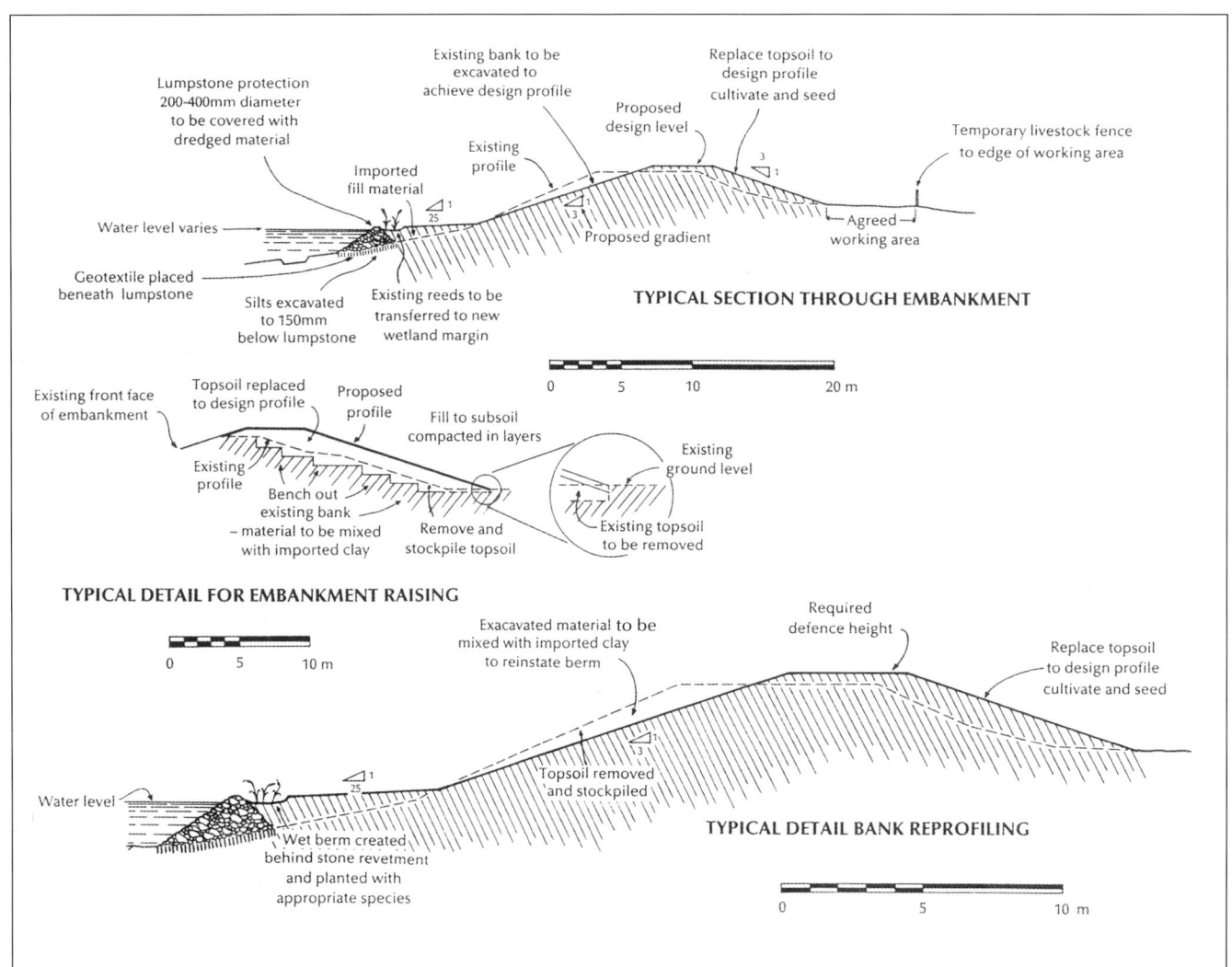

Figure 2 The works involve raising, widening and strengthening the embankments and providing a stone revetment to reduce erosion.
Drawn by D.W. Hopkins, based on an original supplied by the Environment Agency/Bullen Consultants

SETTING THE SCENE

by Steve Catney

Introduction

The Witham Valley Fenland is one of the last, great, relatively unstudied areas, of archaeologically important wetland landscape in the country. These days much archaeological work is, unfortunately, prioritised on the basis of imminent threat to an area (either real or perceived). It was due to such circumstances that discussion between English Heritage and Lincolnshire County Council led to the organisation of a seminar in December 2001 to invite all interested parties to discuss the various archaeological and historical issues in the valley. Papers were invited summarising a declaration of interest in the area, work completed to date, and proposals for future schemes of research. Out of this very successful seminar the Witham Valley Archaeology Research Committee (WVARC) was formed with its first priority being the publication of the proceedings of the seminar. This book is the result of that commitment and aims to raise the profile of the area, by drawing attention to the archaeological work carried out to date and the exciting possibilities that further study of the Witham valley will offer.

This brief introductory paper gives a general background to the study area and previews some of the topics that are dealt with in more detail within this publication. I hope you enjoy reading this volume and are inspired to get involved in any way you can. The archaeology of the Witham valley is a fascinating and professionally challenging subject. However, *Time and Tide* has been produced to enable access to this information for everyone and one of the top priorities for the Witham Valley Archaeology Research Committee is the inclusion of a much wider interest group than professional archaeologists alone (see Start this volume).

Description Of River And Study Area

The river Witham rises as a series of springs bubbling up through the boulder clay capped limestone of the Kesteven uplands, immediately west of the village of South Witham. Except for the river's source and its first few hundred metres, which are just within Leicestershire (O.S. 1998), the whole length of the Witham is within the local authority administrative area of Lincolnshire. It is approximately 140km long, from source to sea. The river flows eastwards from its source before turning north towards Grantham and beyond Grantham it takes a westerly diversion before heading north once again to enter our study area as it meets the Brayford Pool in Lincoln.

At Lincoln the Witham is constrained by, and flows through, a narrow gap (the Lincoln Gap) in the limestone scarp slope known as the Lincoln edge. The gap was created by the river Trent eroding a passage through the limestone as it flowed to the sea because ice sheets to the north had blocked the Humber estuary. The river flows eastwards, its canalised route running close to the northern edge of the valley. The valley is approximately 1.5 km wide immediately east of Lincoln, widening quite rapidly until at Bardney it is approximately 6.5 km wide (see French and Rackham, Fig. 1, this volume) The river turns southeast by Branston Island and holds this course as it flows down to Boston where it meets the Haven and ultimately out into The Wash.

Although the hinterland cannot be ignored, the main study area (to which the remainder of this paper refers) extends for 35km from the Brayford Pool in Lincoln, along the 'Witham Fen', to the confluence with the Kyme Eau and river Bain near Tattershall in East Lindsey, and is contained within the 10 metre contour.

Geography And Geology

At Lincoln the river valley is defined by the Lincoln Gap through the limestone scarp which is approximately 1 km wide. The valley opens up to 1.5 km at Washingborough and is over 6 km wide at Tattershall. The present river is largely contained within the 5 metre contour, while the whole of the valley and the Witham tributaries (Usborne Fig. 1 this volume) is enclosed within the 10 metre contour line. The tributaries include a number of natural but "improved" rivers flowing in from the north (*e.g.* The Bain) and man-made drains joining the Witham from the south (*e.g.* Nocton Delph). The modern river flows along the northern edge of the valley where the land rises relatively steeply to the north. On the northern side the 10 metre contour is within 1 km of the river for much of the area of interest. To the south of the river this same contour is 4-6 km away across a notably flat, farmed, fenland landscape.

The Witham has a complex history of deposition due to glacial and post-glacial deposits, periods of tundra conditions creating significant areas of wind blown sand, the deposition of fluvial silts and sands and the influence of several episodes of sea level rise and marine incursion (see French and Rackham this volume). The sum of all of these effects is a broad valley filled with silts and peats that mask a number of palaeochannels from different periods and a series of sand and gravel bars and islands (see aerial photograph on rear cover).

The uppermost geological strata along the course of the study area are Quaternary drift deposits. The river flows through thick deposits of clayey alluvium within which are peaty laminae (I.G.S 1973), with the uppermost bed being shrunken peat over the majority of the area, almost totally filling up the valley within the 5 metre contour. A number of sand islands, and sand and gravel river terraces protrude through the alluvium and peat. Towards Lincoln and the western edge of the study area, the underlying solid geology is made up of the limestone and clay beds of the dip slope of the Lincoln Edge. Further east the alluvial deposits overlie extensive beds of boulder clay/glacial till while from Potterhanworth downstream they cover substantial marine and estuarine deposits (*ibid.*, B.G.S. 1995, Rylatt 2001). The detailed work being carried out by Rackham (this volume and unpublished) is likely, however, to give greater detail to, and challenge some of, the above geological information, in particular the extent of marine incursion into the valley. To date, marine deposits have been identified by auger survey as far upstream as Fiskerton (pers comm. Rackham)

Recent use of the area for intensive agriculture, the canalisation of the river and its significant improvement in the eighteenth century (Boyes and Russell 1977) and the drainage implemented since the 1940s have resulted in significant shrinkage of the peat and the exposure of some of the buried sand islands. Past marine incursions have also drowned significant areas of woodland, regular reminders of which are seen when 'bog oaks' are dragged from the peat by the plough.

The present canalised river flows between banks standing up to 5 metres high with the river level up to 2.5 metres higher than the surrounding land. The approximate height of the top of the river bank is between 5 - 6 metres O.D. and the average height of the surrounding land is approximately 2 - 2.5 metres O.D. The river channel is some 30 - 35 metres wide; the width of the channel with its flood banks is about 75 metres; if we add the drainage delphs to the north and south of the river, the total width of the complex of channels and banks is approximately 150 metres.

The Archaeology

The computerised Lincolnshire Sites and Monuments Record includes records for 886 monuments and 315 findspots along the entire length of the Witham. Of these, 485 monuments and 205 findspots are located within the study. A significant proportion of the river corridor, including part of the study area, requires the SMR to be brought up to modern standards, a process which will increase the number of computerised records.

The study area is particularly rich in archaeological sites 50 of which are scheduled ancient monuments (see Went this publication), however, it is the number and quality of high status finds that first drew attention to the Witham valley. At first it was tempting to consider that they might all have been casual losses, but the concentration and number of high status items leads one to surmise that there has been a culture of ritual deposition in the Witham spanning many centuries (see Everson and Stocker and Field *et al.* this volume). All periods are represented including Palaeolithic hand axes, Mesolithic flintwork, Bronze Age metalwork, various log boats, the Witham shield, a carnyx, a gold Anglo-Saxon sword hilt and assorted medieval weaponry. As early as the eighteenth century finds were being collected from the river and it is as a direct result of the work of Sir Joseph Banks during the late eighteenth century that many of the finds were recorded and are preserved today.

The finds may be spectacular and offer great opportunity for public display (see Cadbury this volume), but high quality archaeological sites are also widely represented across the valley from as early as the Neolithic (*e.g.* Long Barrow at Catley Priory). It is, however, the proliferation of high quality burial and religious sites that is really intriguing, in particular the monastic sites (see Everson and Stocker this volume). Not only is the number impressive, but also the variety of religious orders and specifically the continuity of focus. Many of the medieval sites are situated immediately adjacent to Bronze Age barrow cemeteries and appear to be linked to causeways across the marsh and open water, the sites of which appear to continue in use over millennia.

In addition to the quality and quantity of archaeology in the Witham valley, the level of preservation is extraordinary. Metal finds emerge from the peat still shiny and with a keen edge; some still have their hafts attached (see Field *et al.* this volume, Fig. 8) and come from very rich palaeo-environmental contexts (see French and Rackham this volume). If all of this was not enough, the significant peat levels protect an inundated valley floor and potentially mask an intact Bronze Age, or even earlier, landscape.

The Challenge

Due to the desiccation and erosion of the peat soils through agricultural practice and flood defence works to protect local inhabitants (see Usborne this volume), along with development-led threats (see Bonnor and Catney this volume) a major challenge is set in place. In addition to these direct threats the area is large, many of the sites obscured and the conservation issues complex (see White this volume).

The Witham Valley Archaeology Research Committee has taken on the challenge of bringing together all of the interests in the valley to create and deliver a management plan for the archaeology of the Witham valley. This is a long-term project which has commenced with the long-term commitment of the agencies, groups and individuals represented on the Committee. The challenge is to identify, record, understand, interpret, promote and protect the Witham Valley Archaeology with long term commitment from all, not least of all the local community who live here.

I hope you enjoy the contributions in this volume. Remember that this is but a start and if you feel you have anything to offer the furtherance of the aims of the WVARC, then we look forward to hearing from you.

Bibliography

Bennett, S. and Bennett, N, (eds), 1993, *An Historical Atlas of Lincolnshire*, (Hull, The University of Hull Press).

British Geological Survey, 1995, 'Horncastle', England and Wales Sheet 115. Solid and drift geology. 1:50,000, (Keyworth, British Geological Survey).

Boyes, J. and Russell, R., 1977, *The Canals of Eastern England*, (London, David and Charles).

Institute of Geological Sciences, 1973, 'Lincoln', Sheet 114, Solid and drift edition, (Southampton Institute of Geological Sciences).

Ordnance Survey, 1998, 'Grantham, Sleaford and Bourne', Landranger, Sheet 130 (Southampton, Ordnance Survey).

Rylatt, J., 2001, *Lower Witham Flood Defence, Part 1: 19 Sections of Flood Defences* (unpublished archaeological desk-based assessment report, Pre-Construct Archaeology).

Simmons, B.B. and Cope-Faulkner, P., 1997, *The Lincolnshire Car Dyke; Past Work, Management Options and Future Possibilities*, (unpublished report 51/97, Archaeological Project Services).

'COMING FROM BARDNEY ...' – THE LANDSCAPE CONTEXT OF THE CAUSEWAYS AND FINDS GROUPS OF THE WITHAM VALLEY

by Paul Everson and David Stocker

Introduction

When Lincolnshire people want someone to shut the door they say (or used to say) 'Dost come from Bardney?' Bardney, it seems, was reputed to have free access, and from most directions the approach was via the causeway that still leads to the modern village across the Witham fen. The ancient saying, however, may have encapsulated an early truth about access to the prominent 'island' on which Bardney stands - it is said to derive from the account of the arrival of the relics of St Oswald here, recounted by Bede (Widdowson 1984, 115; Elder 1997, 55). Until recently, however, the Witham valley has been famous amongst archaeologists, not for its vernacular causeways, but for its spectacular finds of votive metalwork from the river, the best known of which are later prehistoric and early medieval in date. The spectacular prehistoric finds have been the subject of many studies over the years and we will look at their distribution in a moment, but the intention of this paper is to direct some attention back to the causeways that cross the valley at regular intervals. It stresses that the finds and the causeways should be seen together, as different manifestations of past journeys across the fen and, furthermore, that in the medieval era causeways and finds have also to be related to the monastic sites that are prominently placed at the causeways' ends.

The two central reaches of the river Witham extend between the Brayford Pool at Lincoln and its confluence with the rivers Slea and Bain just below Tattershall. The great majority of the famous metalwork finds have been made along these two reaches, and most of the ancient causeways lie between these two points (Fig. 1). The broad valley extends eastwards from Brayford Pool for about 10 km to the confluence with the Barlings Eau, before turning south-east towards Tattershall. Two especially notable features are the embayments at Bardney and at Kyme/Anwick – both the locations of early Christian monasteries. From the late Bronze Age onwards, the rising water levels generated a wetland in the valley floor, characterised by a slow-flowing river in an area of alder-carr fen with many stagnant pools and meres. The 'upland' boundary of the former wetland area is marked today by a peat blanket that fills the valley floor below the 5m contour. Below Lincoln, the modern river channel flows along the north and east sides of the valley and is close to the line of the medieval river. It is thought to have occupied a completely different line, however, closer to the centre of the valley before the medieval period (Wilkinson 1986-7; Lane and Hayes, 1993, 13-4). The causeways mapped probably never blocked the river flow. However, extensive research in Lincoln itself has shown that the Stamp End causeway, at least, influenced water levels upstream and promoted or enhanced existing pools and meres (Jones, Stocker and Vince forthcoming).

Previous Work In The Topic Area

English Heritage (and its predecessors) has so far promoted two major pieces of work on the Witham valley wetlands. The first came in 1981, when Naomi Field made the important discovery of the Fiskerton causeway, and this is discussed in many of the papers that follow, especially that by Mike Parker Pearson and his colleagues. The second, approaching the topic from a landscape perspective, has been focussed on the monastic exploitation of the valley in the medieval period through a study of one monastery in particular – Barlings Abbey.

The Barlings project is a detailed study of one of the most interesting of the medieval monasteries that line the north (that is, Lindsey) bank of the valley in such a remarkable density (Everson and Stocker forthcoming; Stocker and Everson 2002). The Premonstratensian foundation of Barlings is located on the west side of the Bardney embayment, in the angle between the Barlings Eau and the Witham, and on an island named Oxney in the medieval period. It was (and is) linked northwards to the mainland by a causeway approximately 1 km in length.

One aspect of our detailed work on the monastic precinct has enabled us to re-create on paper the substance of the lost conventual church of the abbey, on the basis of its ground plan in the site earthworks, the surviving fragment of standing

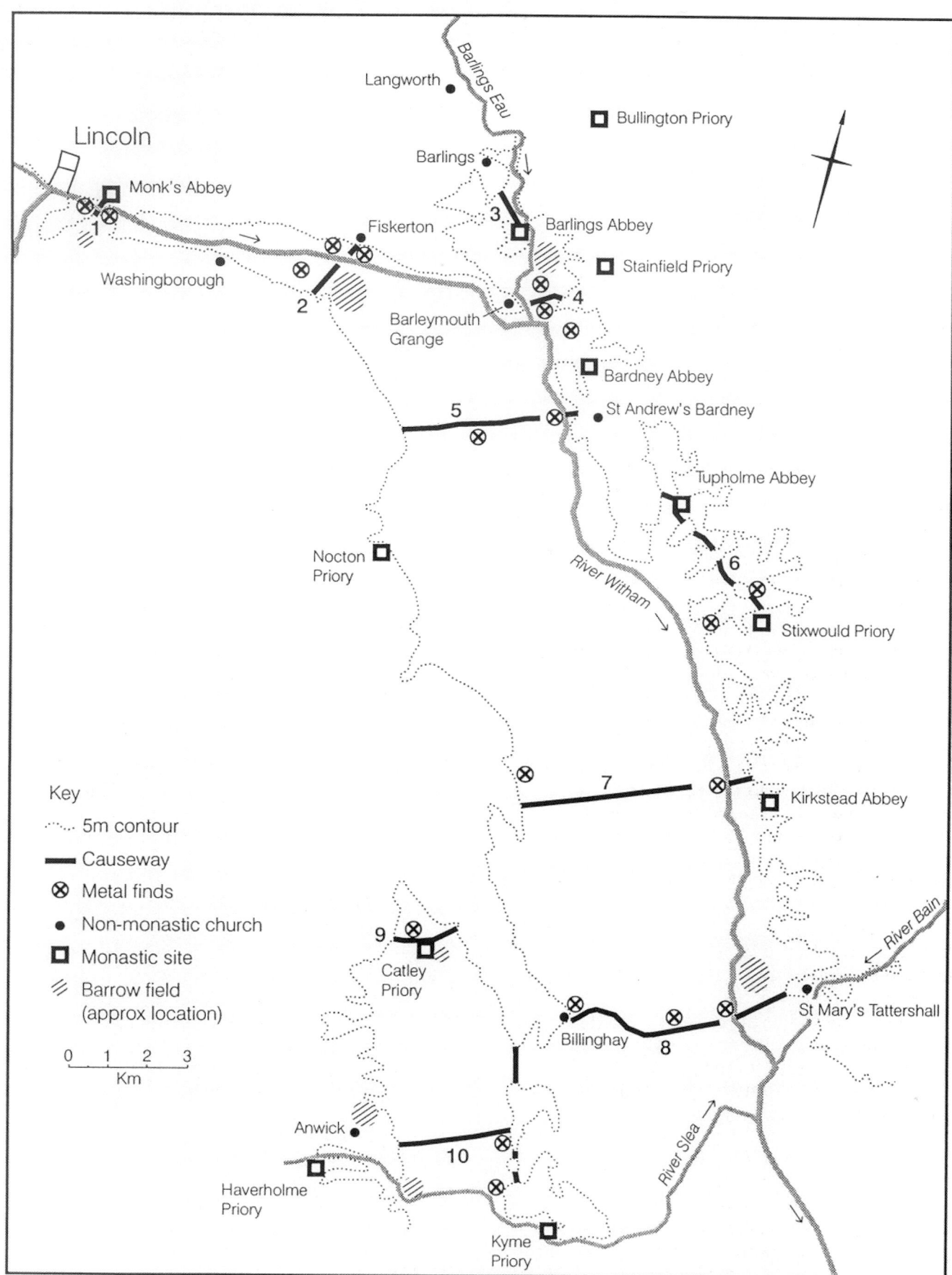

Figure 1 Map showing locations of metal finds, causeways and monastic sites in the central Witham valley.
Drawn by Philip Sinton. © English Heritage

masonry, loose architectural fragments, and early topographical views (Fig. 2). This reconstruction led to the realisation that there was a parochial north aisle within the monastic church, an aisle that served as the parish church. In its turn this directed our attention towards the surviving parish church of St Edward, which is located at the other end of the causewayed access to the abbey. This proves to have been the location of an earlier alien Benedictine priory, founded c.1100 on a pre-existing church, which in turn became part of the endowment of the abbey at its foundation in the mid twelfth century. St Edward's evidently became the chapel of Barlings Abbey's home grange, and re-appeared as the parish church only some time after the Dissolution.

The re-creation of the abbey church also revealed the sheer scale, though not the detail, of the eastern arm of the conventual church as created in the mid fourteenth century. It suggests that the monastic choir was removed wholly east of the crossing, freeing the transeptal space as a grand burial space for the de Lacy Earls of Lincoln, whose Lancastrian kinship with Edward III accounts for the royal funding of these major architectural works. Just such a mausoleum was created at Tattershall a century later for the mighty Lord Cromwell and his family. It was a function shared by most of the Witham monasteries: Kirkstead was the burial place of the twelfth century lords of Tattershall; Bardney Abbey, having initially been the burial place of the saintly king Oswald and of members of the Mercian royal house aspiring to sanctity, was re-founded in the eleventh century as the mausoleum of the

Figure 2 Reconstructed view of the monastic church of Barlings Abbey,
from the north-west.
Drawn by Tony Berry. © English Heritage

powerful de Gant family; and Barlings was founded as the burial place of the de la Hayes, the twelfth century lords of Lincoln Castle. So that many (perhaps all) of these monasteries house – and effectively stand for – the main lordships of Lindsey, whose southern boundary they line and guard.

A second aspect of detailed work on the monastic precinct has identified the site of the sixteenth century palace and its formal setting of gardens occupying the whole precinct, which were created in the wake of the Lincolnshire Rising by Charles Brandon, Duke of Suffolk and brother-in-law to Henry VIII (Everson and Stocker 2003). This development at Barlings at its Dissolution re-emphasises the site's long-term and distinctive status. Furthermore, we have identified links with Charles Brandon's contemporary use of Tattershall Castle and of the abbey site at Kirkstead. This work shows how Brandon's control of and transformation of these special sites was calculated to secure for him symbolic leadership as well as practical rule in the county.

The Barlings project, therefore, has not only delivered a study of a monastic landscape, in terms of the impacts of the creation of a major monastic house on its local area, but it has also brought forward the distinctive long-term significance of the abbey site in the social and political fabric of Lindsey and Lincolnshire. Its location was evidently part of this significance – adjacent to the Bardney embayment, with a large barrow cemetery of 30+ mounds sited immediately to its east within the

Figure 3 Aerial view of Barlings Abbey on the island of Oxney, from the north-west. The causeway to the island is marked by the hedged lane at the bottom of the image; traces of the adjacent barrow cemetery are visible at the top, as earthworks on the near side of the old course of the Barlings Eau and as soilmarks on its far side. See Figure 6. NMR 1866/422, 26-NOV-80. © Crown copyright. NMR

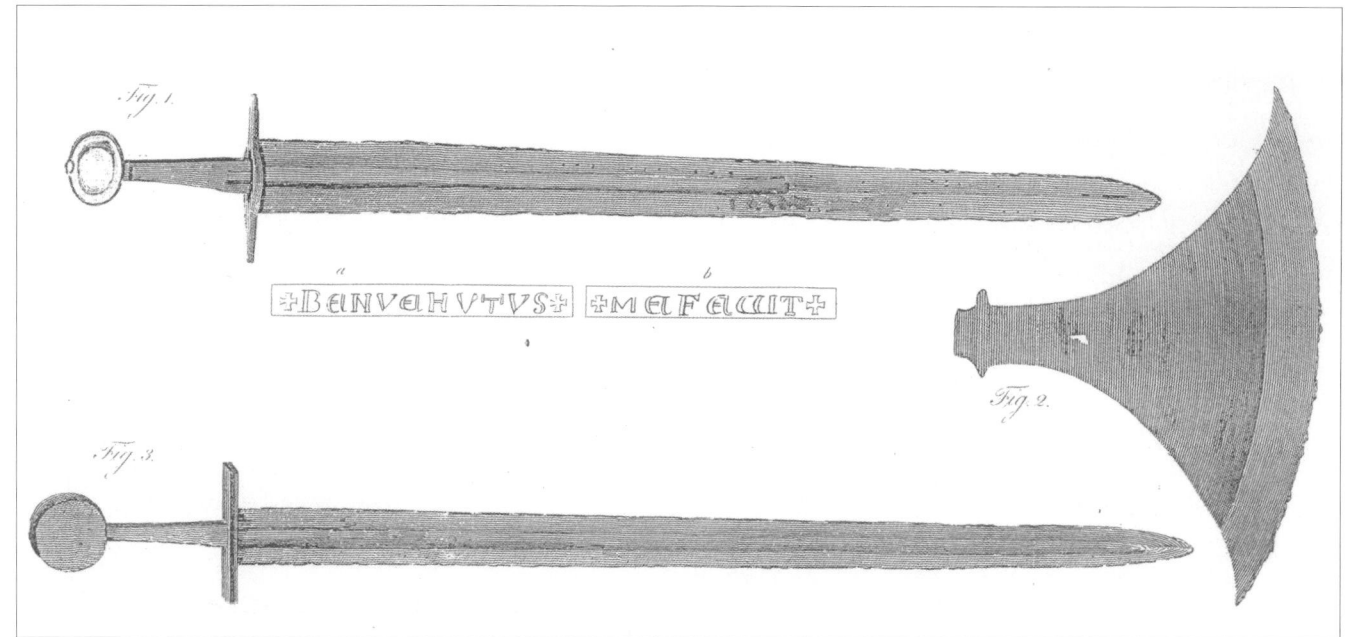

Figure 4 Medieval swords and axe, recovered from the Witham in the late eighteenth century.
Reproduced from Pearson 1796

embayment, and a causeway of unknown antiquity (although at least early medieval origin) leading to it (Figs. 3 and 6). In order to understand this significance more fully, we have collected information about all the Witham valley monasteries, about the causeways that led towards them across the fenlands and about the extensive range of finds which have been discovered in association with them over the past two centuries. The data collected on ten such locations is summarised in Fig. 1.

The catalogue of metalwork finds and other site and artefact-types demonstrates the grouping or clustering of ritual depositions at intervals along the valley. All ten causeways share a striking range of diagnostic characteristics and follow a remarkably consistent pattern, which together strongly suggest that they are pre-monastic in origin. At most of them the archaeological record begins with evidence for an early or middle Bronze Age barrow cemetery on the lower valley sides, presumably located close to the course of the original river. Once the valley had succumbed to inundation and become a landscape of meres and pools in the late Bronze Age and early Iron Age, the sacred significance of these locations started to be marked by a series of votive depositions, predominantly of weapons and other military objects. At most of the sites this sequence of votive depositions seems to have continued through the Iron Age and Romano-British periods and in 70% of cases, deposition continued into the medieval period (Fig. 4). The latest securely dated depositions in these sequences were made in the fourteenth century or later. Typically, neither the prehistoric offerings, nor those of the medieval period, were disabled or 'killed' before deposition. These votive depositions are associated with what later became causeways, but were the causeways constructed at the same time and in association with the votive depositions? Only that at Fiskerton has been excavated and those excavations showed a date of first construction around 600 BC, contemporary with the votive depositions associated with it. We can show that all the causeways (ironically except Fiskerton) already existed by the medieval period, but without excavation it can only be an assumption made on the strength of the finds associated with them that the causeways go back to the late Bronze or early Iron Age. Even so, the similarity between the assemblages from the other causeways and that from Fiskerton is close enough to make entirely credible the suggestion that the medieval causeways may have had such early origins.

As at Barlings, each of these causeways has associated with it a monastic or early church site. The most problematic in this respect is probably the Billinghay-Tattershall example. However, we have argued that the location subsequently occupied by Ralph Cromwell's collegiate church of Holy Trinity was earlier the first site – called 'Kirkstead' – of the great Cistercian abbey of that name (Stocker and Everson 2002; Everson and Stocker forthcoming). The early site here was represented by an isolated church of St Mary, with

Figure 5 View along the Bardney causeway from the west, with St Andrew's Bardney minding the route.
Photo P. Everson

the status of a chapel but with burial rights, which the foundation of Holy Trinity superseded. Presumably this *kirk* was in existence by the time of the formation of the place-name, *i.e.* perhaps between the ninth and eleventh centuries.

Fortunately, in most other cases the presence of an early ecclesiastical site has been more clearly identified. The monastery at Bardney enjoyed the seventh century patronage of the Mercian royal house (Stocker 1993, 107-110) and there is good circumstantial evidence in its early sculpture for an early monastery on the island site at Kyme (*ibid.*, 112-3). Monks Abbey in Lincoln belonged to the Benedictines of St Mary at York when first heard of in the early twelfth century; but there was a tradition – collected by Leland – that it had been the site of the seventh century monastery of *Icanho* mentioned by Bede, and its estate might even have been the medieval successor of a large block of land laid out in the fourth century around the so-called 'villa' at Greetwell Road, Lincoln (Jones, Stocker and Vince forthcoming). The manor of Fiskerton was farmed in demesne throughout the Middle Ages by the Benedictines of Peterborough, after they acquired it in the eleventh century. Their policy of acquiring defunct early church sites in Lincolnshire is best documented with St Chad's ancient monastic estate at Barrow/Barton-on-Humber on the north boundary of Lindsey (Everson and Knowles 1993). At Barlings, too, the ecclesiastical guardian of the causeway was (as we have seen) an alien Benedictine priory founded on a pre-existing church. This pattern lends confidence to the interpretation developed above about an early ecclesiastical site at Tattershall. It is also clear that, for those causeways that cross the Witham valley proper, the causeways' ecclesiastical guardian stands, without exception, at its northern, Lindsey end (Fig. 5).

The location of these early monastic sites at the causeway's end was not due solely to topographical convenience. In a number of cases, obligations of maintenance for the causeways were given to the associated monastic house, probably at their foundation. We know this to have been the case at Bardney Abbey, Tupholme Abbey and Stainfield Priory. Monks Abbey probably had responsibilities for the Stamp End causeway, whilst Peterborough Abbey's Manor at Fiskerton may have been responsible for the ferry at Washingborough-Fiskerton.

There are occasional hints, too, of ceremonies or special practices that took place on the causeways, which may have had their origins in pre-Christian river-based rituals. Medieval fishing rights around the confluence of the Witham and the Barlings Eau belonging to Bardney Abbey were habitually leased to the nuns of Stainfield Priory. The terms of Stainfield's lease specifically permitted the monks of Bardney to visit the grange at Barleymouth – *i.e.* presumably the causeway – to fish the river for one day on the vigil of St Oswald (Stocker and Everson 2002). The specific connection between this ceremonial fishing expedition and the vigil of the saint for whom Bardney was the pre-Viking cult centre makes it highly likely that this was an ancient monastic observance. We may guess that these rituals included casting nets into the river and may wonder whether such ceremonies belong to that large group of pagan festivals that were Christianised in the conversion period. In this case at least, it seems, the connection with the river is explicit.

More important than the rather incomplete documentary evidence for monastic involvement in the maintenance of the causeways that lead towards them, however, is the unambiguous archaeological evidence for the continuation of votive deposition as late as the fourteenth or fifteenth century (Fig. 4; *cf.* White 1979a, b). Furthermore these medieval finds are not rare; in three cases medieval finds outnumber prehistoric ones. In total, causeway zones have produced at least 32 finds of medieval date, including ten swords, five daggers/long knives, six axe-heads and six spearheads. Some of the swords carry incantations inscribed into their blades, which emphasise the superstitious (and presumably ritualistic) character of their depositions.

In brief, we have suggested that the ancient ritual tradition was assimilated by the church and transformed into rites of passage for the founding secular lords, via renewed or re-created causeways, involving deposition of symbols of their lordship (Stocker and Everson 2002). The monasteries acted simultaneously as the symbolic gateways to these lords' land, and as their mausolea: the causeways as the 'straight and narrow road' across the river valley. Finally, the re-focusing of ancient practices onto the Christian sites was completed by the process of enclosure and reclamation of the former wetlands and by the new tradition, from the late fourteenth century, of aristocrats' hanging their military equipment around their tombs – a practice publicly sanctioned by Crown and Church when the armour of Edward the Black Prince was permanently displayed on his tomb in Canterbury Cathedral in 1376.

The Importance Of The Witham Valley For The Topic Area

It can hardly be claimed that locations of riverine votive deposition of prehistoric metalwork and other artefact-types are unique to the Witham or even rare elsewhere. Or even that examples of the conversion of such ancient landscapes by the positioning of early Christian churches is otherwise unrecognised, but they occur (or at least have been understood) in ones and twos. What the central Witham exhibits is a remarkable density of monastic sites, causeways identifiable in the landscape as both standing and buried features, and an extended ritual landscape with a proven time depth. This is exceptional, and of international importance.

The existence of a relatively large body of ancient finds, largely from eighteenth and nineteenth century drainage works, has allowed the patterning of the material to be perceived. Work at Fiskerton has demonstrated the potential of this framework in one location. Further discoveries throughout the valley are inevitable, predictable and will – if tackled in controlled conditions of modern archaeological investigation – allow our understanding to be enormously enriched and refined.

The thesis proposes a Christian conversion at a landscape scale and suggests the purposeful roles of the new rituals in contemporary society. The fact that the Witham valley (of anywhere in western Europe) can sustain the development of these perceptions, in a complex formulation, indicates both the importance of this landscape and its potential to contribute further to new understanding.

The medieval components of this landscape exist in unusual numbers. Specifically, the monastic and early Christian sites are unusually clear and in many cases have excellent preservation in earthwork form. Some of them, like Monks Abbey in Lincoln or Tattershall, derive an additional importance because they are components within complex urban networks. Others, like Stixwould Priory, are almost unknown and have the additional potential of built components. Even where we have architectural survivals of great intrinsic importance, as St Leonard's chapel at Kirkstead, there has been no serious archaeological, as distinct from art historical, discussion of its role within the wider monastic landscape.

Past work at Barlings has shown the sort of densely textured and illuminating insights that can come out of the intelligent study of these sites and how intimately those insights relate to the adjacent wetland landscapes. In addition to Barlings, preliminary work on the sixteenth century aspects of both Tattershall and Kirkstead has confirmed that those sites too can contribute in different ways to the overall picture.

Nor should we omit (in excitement at the rich artefactual assemblages of the wetlands) the proper need to understand the processes and circumstances whereby these ancient landscapes passed away and were transformed into latter-day

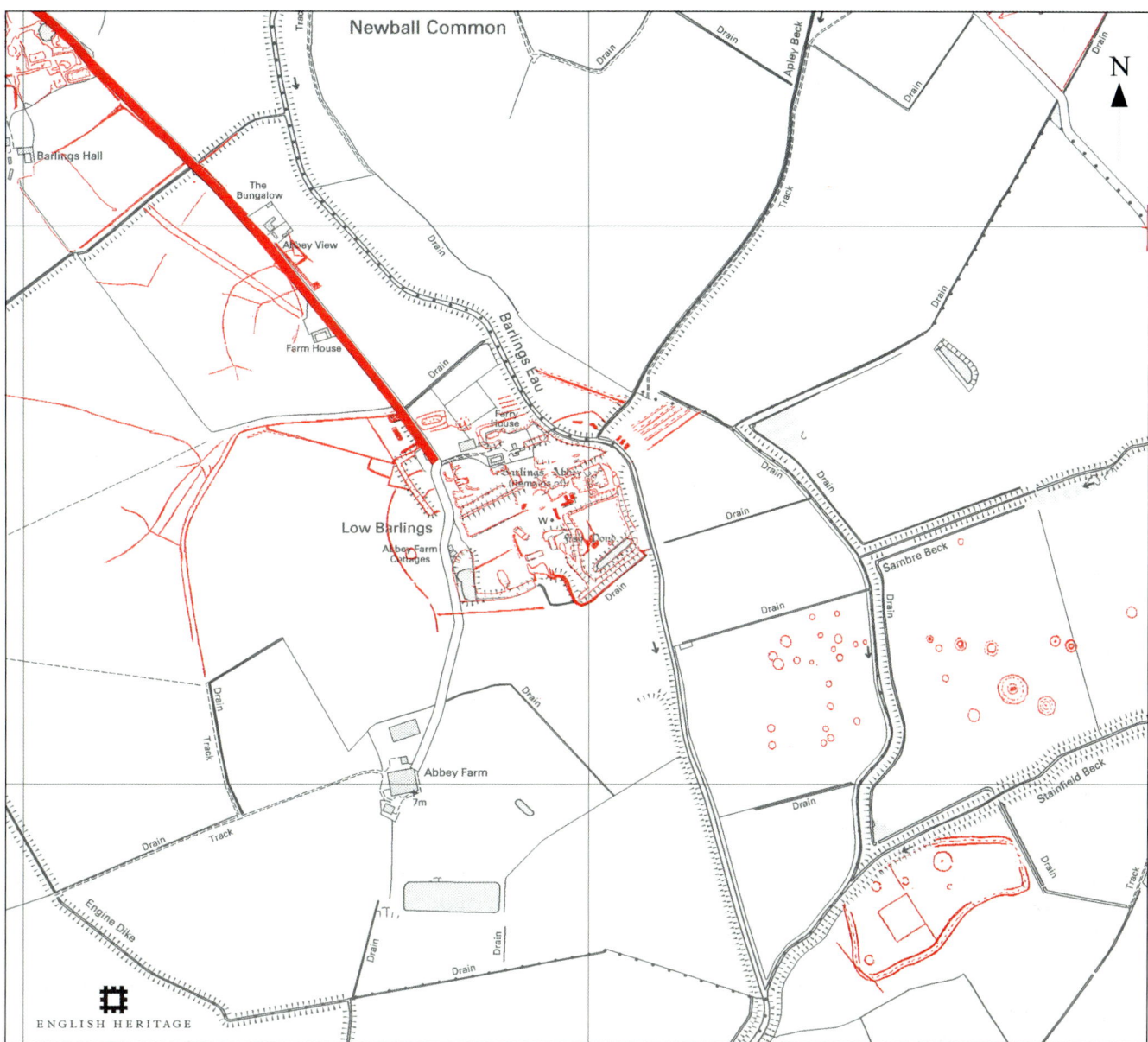

Figure 6 Extract from NMP mapping, sheet TF 07 SE, with the causeway added as a linear antiquity (NMP data shown in red). This shows the characteristic grouping of monuments at Barlings, focused on the island in the embayment. © Crown copyright. NMR. The map base is reproduced from the OS map by English Heritage with the permission of Ordnance Survey on behalf of The Controller of Her Majesty's Stationery Office, © Crown copyright. All rights reserved. Unauthorised reproduction infringes Crown Copyright and may lead to prosecution or civil proceedings. Licence Number GD03085G

enclosed and cultivated landscapes in the central Middle Ages. Nothing would have made so effective a symbol of the triumph of the new church over the old religion as the construction of a causeway across the formerly sacred pools!

Very usefully, much of the Witham valley was covered by National Mapping Programme (NMP) mapping through the recent Lincolnshire project (Fig. 6; see Bewley 1998). That makes it all the more urgent for that part of the valley that fell outside that programme to be done, too. The Witham landscape also benefits from the results of the Urban Archaeological Database/Urban Archaeological Assessment programme at Lincoln (Jones, Stocker and Vince forthcoming), which encompasses one of the causeways and other features (such as a possible early church site at Hartsholme, apparently linked to Bardney) of relevance to the wider valley. Through work in the city of Lincoln, also, there is a well-developed grasp on medieval and later ceramics, and other materials, that can underpin work on finds groups. The collection of pottery from Short Ferry, which is of exceptional quality and interest (White 1976), is a prime candidate.

THE FISKERTON CAUSEWAY: RESEARCH - PAST, PRESENT AND FUTURE

by Naomi Field, Mike Parker Pearson and Jim Rylatt

Introduction

The timber causeway at Fiskerton is one of a handful of excavated watery deposition sites in Europe which together provide a fascinating insight into important aspects of Iron Age religion and culture. In 1981 and again in 2001 archaeological excavations on the north bank of the river Witham revealed three north-south lines of timber posts in association with a spread of Iron Age and Roman metalwork, pottery and bone. The precise dating of the causeway has been possible through dendro chronological analysis of the causeway timbers. The associated metalwork finds are of the La Tène style, but the Fiskerton finds are earlier than those from both La Tène (Vouga 1923) and the classic Welsh site of Llyn Cerrig Bach on Anglesey (Fox 1947 which establishes it as one of the earliest structures in Europe belonging to the La Tène period). The first Fiskerton monograph - on the 1981 excavation - is currently being published (Field and Parker Pearson in press) and a second volume is intended for the 2001 excavation.

The river Witham has produced many Iron Age metal finds, second only in quantity to those from the Thames (Fitzpatrick 1984). This is undoubtedly due to the eighteenth and nineteenth century programmes of embanking and dredging of the river below Lincoln, especially during 1787-8. It was thanks to the fortuitous presence of antiquarians that many of the artefacts recovered from these works survive to this day. Much of the credit goes to Sir Joseph Banks, President of the Royal Society, who lived at Revesby Abbey near Boston and also had a house not far from the Witham in Horncastle.

Until the eighteenth century the Witham valley remained largely undrained and a thick layer of peat had accumulated in the valley bottom. The shrinkage and erosion of the peat resulting from nearly 250 years of drainage works have transformed the character and environment of the valley. The stretch of river between Lincoln and Bardney was straightened and canalised from 1812 and large numbers of finds were made at Washingborough in 1816, and during the construction of the lock at Bardney. In addition to the metal artefacts, nineteen log boats have been recorded from along the course of the Witham, with a large concentration at Short Ferry, about a mile east of the Fiskerton causeway.

Ancient Discoveries Which May Have Come From The Fiskerton Causeway Or Its Vicinity

Of the many finds recovered from the river, a number may have been found at or close to the Fiskerton causeway. An anthropoid-hilted dagger with its pommel apparently carved as a Lincoln imp, found in 1787 and recorded as probably from near Fiskerton, was last seen in 1863. The famous Witham bronze shield, with its boar motif and central coral-studded boss (front cover illustration), is recorded as being found below Lincoln in 1826 probably from the immediate vicinity of Washingborough/Fiskerton. The Witham scabbard of gilt bronze and another Iron Age sword are thought to have been among finds in 1826 from below the Stamp End lock in Lincoln and potentially from the Washingborough/Fiskerton area. Two iron swords in bronze scabbards from Washingborough were exhibited to the Royal Archaeological Institute's meeting in Lincoln in 1848 but have since been lost. There has been some confusion about the findspot of the famous Tattershall Ferry bronze *carnyx* or 'war trumpet' found around 1768 (Piggott 1959; Hunter 2001), erroneously attributed by Cyril Fox to the Fiskerton ferry. Unfortunately this instrument was melted down in an early scientific experiment to determine the composition of prehistoric metals (Pearson 1796).

The Discovery Of The Causeway

The modern Witham is embanked and flanked by two drains, the North and South Delphs, into which flow a network of perpendicular drains. In 1978 the North Delph was dredged and recut, and upon weathering, exposed two lines of staggered posts running north-south. In June 1980 Vernon Stuffins, who was metal detecting on his mother's land, was attracted to the area by the posts and found various items including a La Tène I sword in its scabbard. Mr Stuffins also found four openwork bronze mounts inlaid with studs, later identified as coral. These formed part of a remarkable Early La Tène

The Fiskerton Causeway: Research Past, Present and Future by N Field, M Parker Pearson and J Rylatt

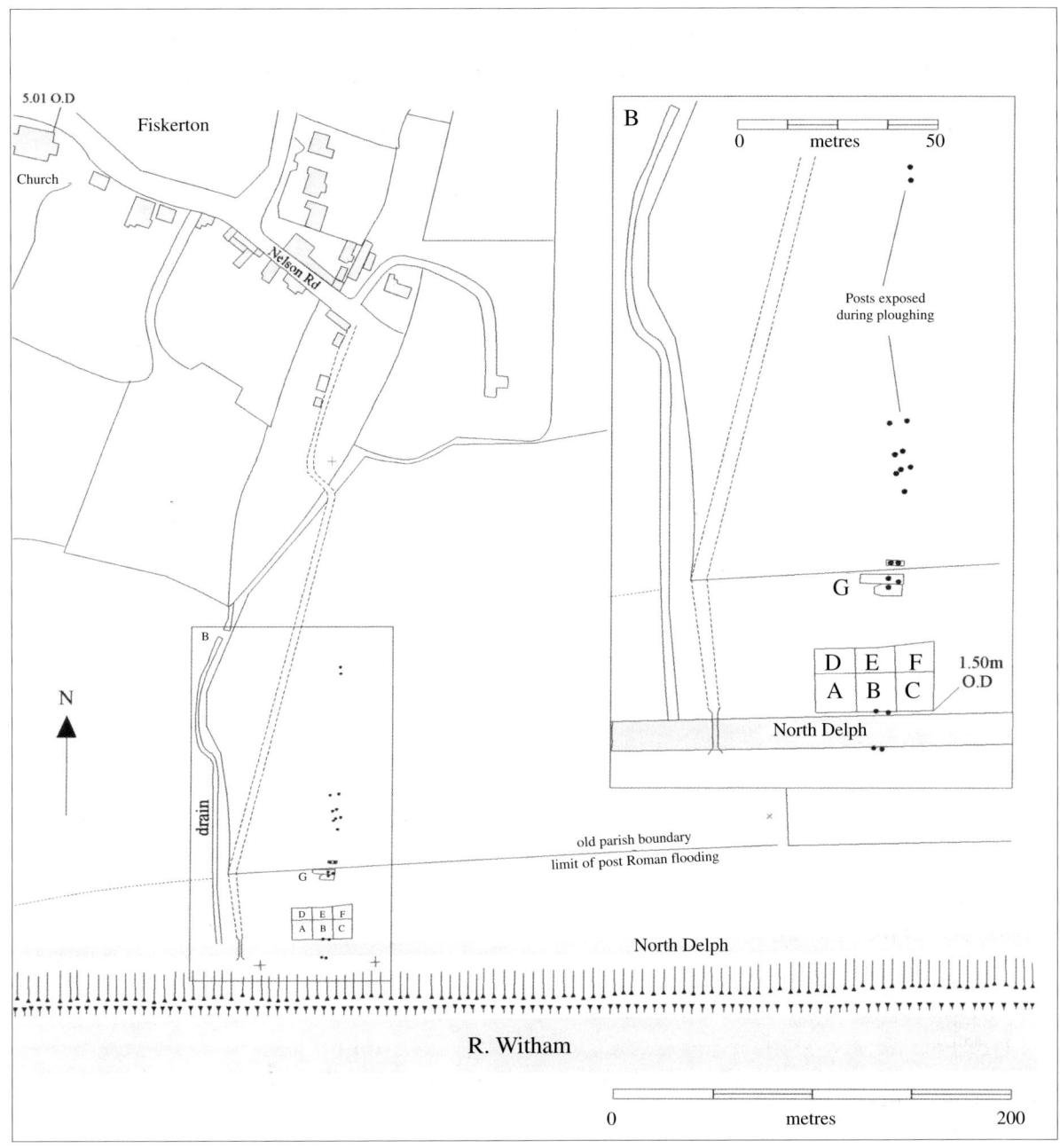

Figure 1 Trench location and setting of the 1981 excavation.
Adapted from M. Williams, based on survey by M. Clark

sword hilt although it was some years before being identified as such. The finds were taken for identification to the City and County Museum in Lincoln. In December 1980 the North Lincolnshire Archaeological Unit was asked to conduct a trial excavation adjacent to the North Delph and the site of the finds. This established that the timber posts continued from the bank of the North Delph northwards into the adjacent field. A well-preserved timber structure of any date would have been of interest but the chance that it could be Iron Age - and provide for the first time a context for some of the high-quality metalwork from the Witham - gave the site a special significance.

The 1981 Excavation

It was with great expectation that a twelve week season of work began in June 1981, funded by the Department of the Environment's Inspectorate of Ancient Monuments. It was the intention to spend two or three seasons on the site, however, funding

Figure 2 General view of the 1981 excavations.
Photo N. Field

did not continue beyond the first season and the investigation of the site remains incomplete.

An area straddling the post-alignment, was stripped of topsoil and was sub-divided into six equal-sized blocks each 10m square (Fig. 1 Areas A-F). Only Areas B, E and F were fully excavated below the base of the topsoil. Two small trenches (Trench G and the 'machine trench') were examined to the north of the main excavations and limited recording was undertaken in a small area (Trench H) on the south bank of the North Delph (Fig. 4).

Two rows of north-south aligned posts, 2.4m apart, ran through the east side of Areas B and E, forming the main structure on the site (Fig. 2). In all, 87 posts in the west row and 82 in the east were exposed, which formed six main clusters each about 3m apart. There was also a third row of nineteen posts, 6m to the west of the double post row.

After ploughing to the north of the excavation area, further posts were observed. The posts ran for at least 160m in a north-northeasterly direction, towards the modern village of Fiskerton. Posts were also detected on the south side of the North Delph where a further eight were recorded. Excavations in the summer of 2001 revealed more of the causeway south of this area. The 1981 excavations thus uncovered only a tiny part of this timber structure.

The posts were mainly of oak and alder, and their diameters ranged between 0.1m and 0.2m. One of the posts recorded in the machine trench to the north of the main excavations was pulled out with a mechanical excavator and found to be 5m in length. Another post which had fallen over was fully excavated and proved to be much shorter at about 2m in length. The tips of both posts were sharpened to a fine point.

Large quantities of worked horizontal timbers, many of them notched planks, were found between the posts in a layer of black silt containing wood chips and twigs. Five planks were found in Area B and of the 39 worked horizontal timbers lying between the causeway posts in Area E (Fig. 3), ten were planks. To the east of the posts in Area F was the best preserved and longest plank of all, with peg holes at each end. In amongst the posts were *in situ* pegs and stakes, all of which were of much smaller dimensions than the posts (typically 2-5cm in cross-section). They may have been used to secure the horizontal planks in position, but none was found in association. The timber causeway fell into decay and possibly collapsed. This layer of timbers may also represent the actual demolition of the causeway. These horizontal timbers were then covered with a metalled surface of limestone rubble. The area was subsequently sealed by a thick layer of flood silts.

The Form Of The Timber Causeway

Interpretation of the timber posts presents two considerable problems. One is how we establish from what stratigraphic level they were inserted into the river silts. The other is what sort of superstructure these posts supported. The level at which the causeway was constructed is made problematic because of the possible scouring action of the river and the removal of certain layers within the Iron Age and Roman periods.

The tops of the posts have long since rotted away and we have little idea of their original lengths, except that at least some were as much as 5m in length. The posts must have been driven into the silt and peaty mud of the riverbed but presumably they would have continued to sink even deeper if they had supported traffic over a continuous period. In recent years the shrinkage of peat in the riverine sediments has caused the deposits around the posts to fall in height so the relationship of the horizontal and vertical elements of the structure may have considerably altered over time.

Did the posts support a bridge-like raised walkway of horizontal planks, or were they part of a seasonally submerged and low-lying trackway in which horizontal timbers were pinned down on top of the river silts? The balance of evidence from the 1981 excavation points to interpretation as a

Figure 3 Part of the causeway (Area E) excavated in 1981. Upright posts and horizontal timbers are clearly visible with a section of limestone rubble left in situ at the north (top right on photo) end of the trench. Photo N. Field

low causeway rather than a raised walkway, for the following reasons:

- The timber rows are wholly unlike those of the putative bridges at La Tène and other Iron Age Alpine sites. They have no angled or raked timbers to provide buttress supports, and there is no evidence for crossbeams to tie the opposing posts of the causeway together for greater strength.

- Although there was no pegged-down planking, there were contexts in which pegs remained *in situ*. While the regular replacement of horizontal planks and timbers would have been made impossible by the forest of upstanding existing posts this may not have been a problem if the tops of the posts were close to the surface of the peat prior to its shrinkage, or sawn off when they became redundant.

- The limestone metalling which replaced the decayed timbers must surely have been set on a ground surface.

Dendrochronological Dating Of The Posts

Dendrochronological analysis demonstrated that the construction sequence of the rows of timbers can be separated out into a series of at least nine phases spanning a period of 167 years after 457/456 BC. The last dated timber posts were erected after 321 BC and probably before 282 BC. Of the third row of posts to the west, only one was suitable for dendrochronology, producing a felling date of

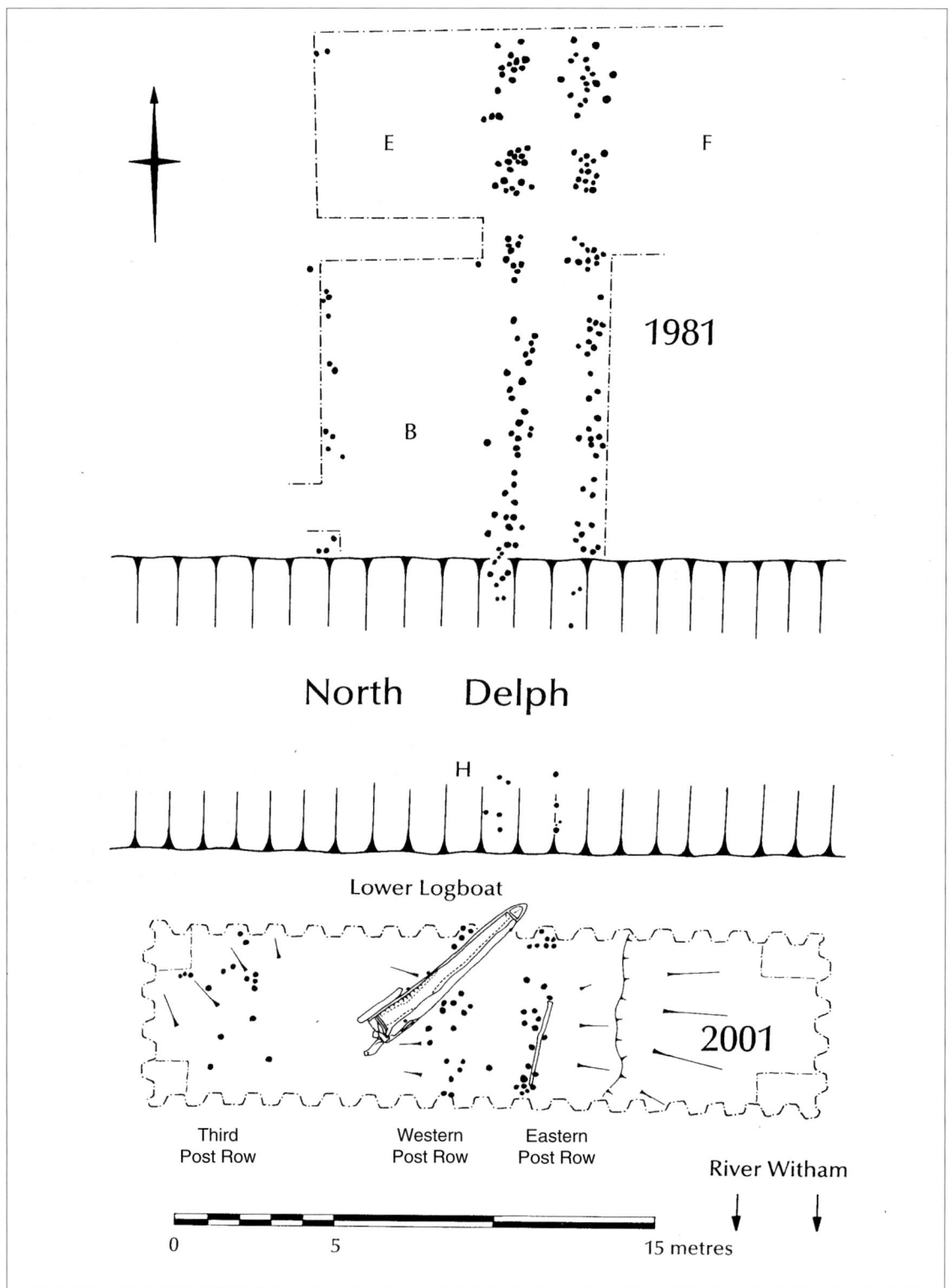

Figure 4 Composite plan of the 1981 and 2001 excavations showing the post rows and other main features.
Adapted by D.W. Hopkins from drawings by N. Field and J. Rylatt

385 BC which did not tally with the felling dates of the causeway posts. This third alignment could have acted as a 'groyne' to protect the causeway when the flooded river was in full spate, or provided points to tie up boats, or have provided greater solidity in the deeper water, similar to the additional rows in the middle of the Flag Fen timber alignment (Pryor 2001).

Earlier Timber Structures

Two timber structures on different alignments to the post rows were found at the base of the stratigraphic sequence. One consisted of two parallel rows of wattling, 0.5m apart and at least 2.4m long, which had been cut through by the posts. At least four layers of horizontal twigs were exposed but the base was not located. Its southeast-northwest alignment was similar to that of a curvilinear spread of twigs immediately to the west of the causeway's posts which ran along the full length of Area B, in silts below the level of the wattling. Eight stake holes filled with mixtures of crushed shell, moss and twigs were also found in the silt deposits along the western side of the causeway. The stakes were removed prior to the formation of peat which lay beneath the horizontal timbers of the causeway. It is unfortunate that so little of the site was excavated to this depth and the full extent and date of these earlier features is not known.

The 1981 Finds

Iron Age Martial Equipment

The artefacts deposited beside and under the causeway form a remarkable group of 167 objects dated on typological grounds to the Iron Age and the later Roman period. They include a coral-inlaid bronze sword handle, two swords in iron scabbards, a short sword and pieces of a fifth and sixth sword. Three swords can be assigned more specifically to La Tène I, in the fifth and fourth centuries BC. Five of the swords are undecorated but the bronze sword handle is an extraordinary item of anthropoid shape with decorated bronze finials and plaques, coral-inlaid discs and domed studs. It probably dates to the second half of the fourth century BC and, though unparalleled in Britain, can be compared with two East European examples from Kysice in Bohemia, and Liebau in Germany (Stead 1996: 22; in press).

Other military items include eleven iron spearheads most of which were very corroded and fragmentary. The 55 bone 'gouges' from the site are best interpreted as spearheads on the basis of comparable finds elsewhere in Britain and Europe, although not one of these was hafted and microwear analysis revealed multiple uses (Olsen in press).

A bronze roundel, whose central cut-out motif contains a dome of 'sealing-wax red' glass, may have once been attached by three bronze rivets to a shield. Roundels on the Battersea shield, and from Lexden in Essex, and Hertford Heath, have red glass pressed into the underside of domed bronze frames in this way but the semi-tubular border of the Fiskerton roundel more closely resembles the slightly larger pieces from Bugthorpe, east Yorkshire, which were also thought to be shield ornaments (Stead 1985: 16-17, 34; 1979: 58; in press). More recently two similar roundels, slightly smaller than the Fiskerton example, and with coral ornament, have been found in a Wetwang Slack cart-burial where they seem to have been attached

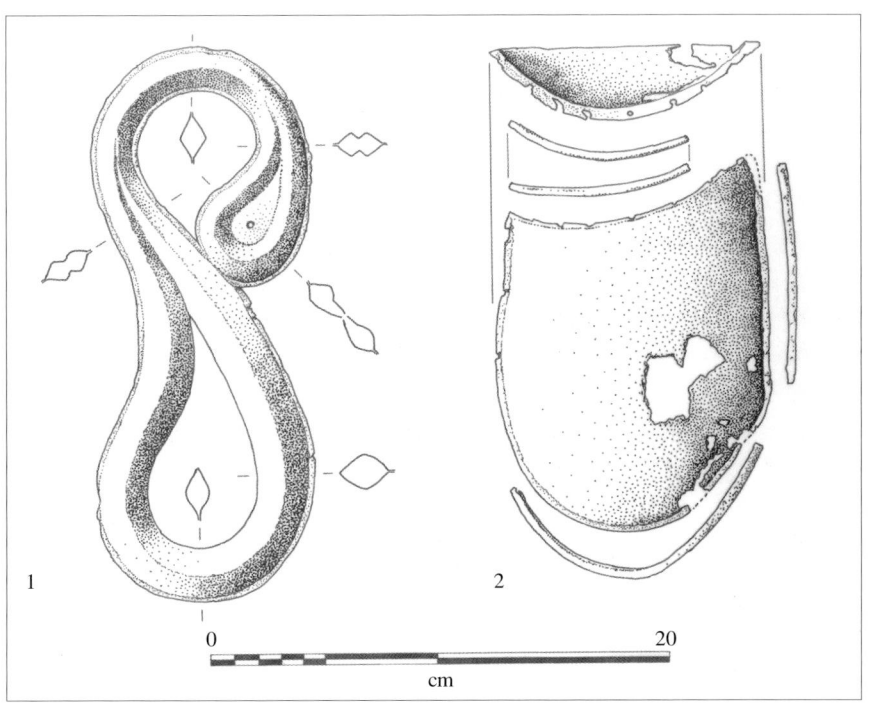

Figure 5
Finds from the 1981 excavation included this 'S' shaped bronze article of unknown function (left) and a curved piece of bronze sheet (right) which may have formed an epaulette for a robe or cloak.
Adapted by D.W. Hopkins from drawing by M. Clark

to a sword-belt (Dent 1985). Another possible shield fitting consists of eight fragments (four joining) of a decorative circular mount, four inches in diameter. Three rivet holes survive, indicating that the mount was attached to a flat plate. The surfaces are tinned. The crimped central rib is reminiscent of part of the mount on the Witham shield.

A curved piece of bronze sheet (Fig. 5), superficially resembling a shoulder-piece, was found immediately west of the double row of posts. Its narrow horizontal flange has holes for five rivets or pins. Three joining lengths of bronze binding were associated. Celtic body armour - other than chainmail - is unknown and there is nothing else like it in the Roman repertoire. It may have formed an epaulette attached to a robe or cloak.

A bronze figure-of-eight (S-shape) of unknown function (Fig. 5) was found set vertically between the double post row. It is unique, presenting no evidence of its purpose. It is made of sheet bronze and comprises two complementary sides tightly riveted together to form a tubular outline 10mm-14mm deep. The overall shape is bordered by a flange through which the two sides are linked by rivets. There seems to be no wear to give a clue to the function of this S-shape, and no means of attachment to anything (unless by the rivet in the smaller lobe, which seems unlikely).

Other Iron Age Finds

As well as military items there were metal and woodworking tools including two metalworking hammerheads, four metalworking files, three shaft-hole axes, two woodworking files (one with a decorated antler handle). The wave-tendril motif on this handle is in the 'Waldalgesheim Style' of the late fourth to early third century BC (Stead 1996: 22; in press).

Another unique item from the site was an iron pull-saw with a decorated blade and antler handle. The two surviving blade fragments have been decorated on both sides and the item probably dates to the late third century BC.

There were two iron linchpins, an iron reaping hook, a jet ring and two amber beads. Both beads have internal dog-toothed grooves and bevelled edges. They are so far unmatched on account of their unusual facetting, making them very different from the doughnut-shaped amber beads from other British Iron Age sites. While a Roman date for these beads cannot be ruled out, as with the Iron Age comparisons, there is nothing similar to their internal fluting from Roman assemblages. Fragments of at least sixteen Iron Age pots were found on the site including two almost complete vessels which can be dated from their position in relation to a dendrochronologically dated post to after 375/374 BC.

Amongst the animal bones of cattle, sheep, pig, horse, red deer, dog and beaver were three fragments of human bone. Radiocarbon dating of two of the human bones confirmed their Iron Age attribution, to the same time period of the fourth-third centuries BC as many of the Iron Age artefacts. The most interesting fragment was part of an adult male's skull bearing a peri-mortem chop mark at the back of the head, probably inflicted with a sword.

Roman Finds

After a gap of as long as 250 years, during the second and first centuries BC, the site of the ruined causeway was used between the late first century AD and the fourth century AD for the deposition of Roman items. These included two Irchester-type bronze bowls, three whetstones and eleven pots. A wooden strut probably derives from a Roman boat.

The Excavation In 2001

In the year 2000 the Environment Agency embarked upon a five-year programme to enhance specific sections of the flood defences of the river Witham and its tributaries between Lincoln and Boston. Pre-Construct Archaeology (Lincoln) was commissioned to monitor the groundworks during the initial phase of this programme. This first component of the Lower Witham Flood Defence Improvement Scheme included the section of the northern bank of the river that runs immediately to the south of Fiskerton.

The excavations undertaken in 1981 had identified a number of vertical posts on the southern edge of the North Delph, which suggested that the Iron Age causeway continued southwards beneath the modern canalised river channel (Field and Parker Pearson in press). Consequently, an evaluation trench was opened, and this confirmed the presence of the causeway.

Figure 6 General shot of the causeway under excavation, looking east. The tops of the two post rows can be seen running along the top of the image, with the limestone rubble concentrated on the western side of the structure. The bow of the lower logboat was removed before the sheet piling was inserted, but the stern can just be seen protruding from the rubble at the centre of the image. Photo J.Rylatt

The enhancement of the riverbank involved the removal of the topsoil, followed by the deposition and compaction of imported clay along its outer edge. The County Archaeologist considered it likely that these works would compress the underlying peat and distort or damage *in situ* archaeological deposits. As a result the Environment Agency agreed to fund the full excavation of the section of the causeway lying within the footprint of the enlarged bank. The strip of land between the existing flood bank and the North Delph is only 8m wide, the archaeological excavation of which created an interesting technical and health and safety problem, which was overcome through the use of sheet piling (see Fig. 6). This restricted the investigation to a 5m wide section of the causeway. The trench was opened at the end of July 2001 and excavation continued until the middle of September. The post-excavation analysis is still in its early stages, therefore, it is only possible to provide an interim account of the results of this second intrusive investigation.

Stripping of the topsoil exposed the tops of a number of vertical timbers, thereby indicating the location and orientation of the two rows of posts forming the causeway (Figs. 4 and 6). Excavation rapidly established that all of the post-Roman deposits had been removed. The deposit immediately beneath the topsoil on the eastern side of the causeway was found to contain a number of Roman pots. These were only partially complete, as the upper portion of each had been 'sliced off' during the removal of the overlying sediments. This probably occurred during the embankment of the river in the nineteenth century.

The Uppermost Logboat

The deposit containing the Roman vessels sealed a layer of organic mud which enveloped a substantial horizontal timber protruding from the section at the north-east corner of the trench. Excavation demonstrated that this was the bow and bilge of a dugout logboat, which had exceeded 7m in length. This vessel was poorly preserved and may have been partially exposed during the nineteenth century groundworks, its stern subsequently being removed by the creation of the North Delph.

The organic mud had accumulated over a layer of tabular limestone rubble. The stones had been laid along the causeway, both between the two rows of posts and along their margins. On the eastern side of the structure, the rubble had been deposited upon a timber framework. The latter comprised a lattice of larger branches, upon which smaller branches and brushwood had then been placed.

Excavation demonstrated that much of the limestone had sunk, or been trampled, into earlier deposits.

Beneath the limestone and timber surface there was a localised deposit of well-fired charcoal, which was situated between the post rows and extended from one edge of the trench to the other. While some pieces of charcoal were evidently derived from small branches, others were very large. This raises the possibility that a fire had destroyed any superstructure that may have been associated with this section of the causeway, and could, therefore, explain why the excavation of 2001 did not expose large horizontal timbers comparable to those discovered in 1981.

Figure 7 The bow portion of the lower logboat which was excavated and lifted prior to the insertion of the sheet piling surrounding the excavated area. The bow was wedged tightly between two clusters of posts in the eastern row, with the centre of the starboard side resting against posts in the western alignment.
Photo S. Catney

The Lower Logboat

Removal of the limestone also revealed one of the more outstanding artefacts recovered during the excavation. This was a second logboat, which was in a far better state of preservation than the first (Fig. 7). It was 7.2m long and had a rounded bow. The vessel was fitted with a stern board, which sat in a shallow groove cut into the bilge and was sealed with puddled clay. The tops of the gunwales were level with the uppermost components of the rubble layer, while the basal fill of the vessel contained a lens of charcoal. This burnt material was comparable to that found elsewhere between the posts, indicating that the boat was already in this position prior to the conflagration.

The front half of the logboat lay diagonally across the causeway. Its bow was wedged tightly between two clusters of posts in the eastern row, with the centre of the starboard side resting against posts in the western alignment. Vertical timbers did not abut the corresponding section of the port side, indicating that the boat could have worked free if moving water ever surrounded this section of the causeway. To prevent this happening, two stakes had been hammered into the underlying clay. Additionally, a large branch had been rested against the rear half of the port side, and a large chunk of oak was wedged against the stern. This wedge came from the bole of the tree and had been worked to produce a facetted surface of greater complexity than necessary to merely hold the boat in place. It has been suggested that this item could have been a wooden anvil.

Examination of the underside of the logboat indicated that it was completely covered by fresh tool marks. This suggests that the vessel had been barely used, if ever, at the time that it was incorporated into the causeway. Together, this pristine condition and the evidence for careful and deliberate placement clearly suggest that this boat represents yet another valuable item selected for votive deposition at the causeway. The patterns of axe marks suggest that the boat was fashioned by two rows of boatbuilders working along either side of it (Maisie Taylor, *pers comm.*).

Woodworking

Removal of the charcoal layer and the logboat exposed a spread of wood chips and bark in the area contained between the post rows. This material appears to be the residue of on-site woodworking relating to the construction or repair of the causeway. The wood chips lay upon a thin brushwood surface that had been secured with small roundwood pegs, and it is likely that it had been laid to facilitate the causeway's construction. The brushwood lay directly upon the surface of the clay subsoil, a relationship suggesting that any vegetation or peaty deposits had been cleared from the line of the causeway prior to its construction.

A total of 45 posts were exposed in the two rows forming the causeway, with an additional post situated on the centre line of the structure near the southern edge of the trench. Most of these posts had been used in a relatively unmodified form, with the bark still attached. A few of the larger timbers had been radially split or had worked surfaces. Only one post had a surviving joint. This notch was cut into the top of a bulbous scar on the side of the timber. However, as the top of the timber had been inserted into the ground, the notch faced downward, possibly suggesting that it had been incorrectly placed or that the timber had been reused. On the final day of the excavation a number of posts were extracted. This demonstrated that the timbers were all relatively straight and were still approximately 3m long. Their ends were extremely well made, each tapering from approximately 1m to a sharp point.

The 'third row' of posts was also exposed during the excavation. As previously identified in 1981, this lay six metres to the west of the causeway. However, the section examined in 2001 differed morphologically from the element seen before, as it splayed to become two rows during its progress toward the southern edge of the trench. A lattice of horizontal coppice poles, all extremely straight and up to three metres long, surrounded this additional post row. None of the poles were joined, either to each other or to the posts. Yet the close spatial relationship between these vertical and horizontal timbers suggests that the poles may represent the remains of a collapsed superstructure.

The Iron Age Artefacts

In addition to the two logboats, a number of other remarkable artefacts were recovered during the excavation. Some of these items were amazingly well preserved. An iron dagger found against the western edge of the causeway was still sharp, its naked tang suggesting that the handle had been removed prior to deposition. A sword, the tip of which appears to have been broken off in antiquity, lay close to the dagger. Numerous pieces of bronze - 'U'-section metal binding, decorated strips and two roundels - were also recovered and may represent components of sheaths associated with these or similar weapons. An almost complete, hafted spear was also recovered (Fig. 8). It had an iron head and a thin wooden shaft, a smooth dowel 0.01m in diameter and was approximately 2m long.

An iron looped and socketed axe, still containing half of a two-part haft, was found among the wood chippings and brushwood at the base of the deposits (Fig. 9), perhaps relating to the building of the causeway or even to a previous structure. It lay adjacent to the disarticulated, but virtually complete remains of a young pig, their context raising the possibility that both represented dedicatory deposits. The axe was evidently a skeuomorph of Later Bronze Age examples and may be dated to the later eight or seventh century BC. If the brushwood is part of an earlier structure (along with the wattling and twig deposit found in the 1981 excavation) then the axe may derive from pre-causeway Early Iron Age activity. If the

Figure 8
The near complete Iron Age spear during excavation. The spearhead is situated to the left, with the slender dowel shaft running right up to the steel piling. The bottom part of the shaft was subsequently recovered from the other side of the cofferdam.
Photo J. Rylatt

Figure 9 The socketed iron axe, which was deposited within a layer of wood chips and brushwood. Also visible are bones representing the remains of a juvenile pig. It is possible that both the axe and the pig represented foundation deposits made at the time that the causeway was initially constructed in 457/6 BC. Photo J. Rylatt

brushwood was part of the construction of the earliest post rows then it was presumably already an heirloom at the time the causeway was initially constructed in 457/6 BC.

An iron file with an antler handle was also discovered in the area contained between the two rows of posts, while a complete spindle, the wooden peg still passing through the stone whorl, had been deposited to the east of the causeway. It was also evident that a large number of unmodified, rounded pebbles had been carried along the causeway and dropped along its margins. It is tempting to see the latter as representing some form of ritual observance relating to the more mundane tasks of routine activity.

A preliminary comparison of the results obtained in 1981 and 2001 indicates that there are differences in the distribution of the various artefact types. For example, only two bone spearheads ('gouges') were found in 2001, in contrast to the 55 recovered in 1981. This suggests that different types of votive offering were deposited in a deliberate and highly structured way.

During the machine trenching to evaluate deposits on either side of the causeway prior to the 2001 excavation, an iron currency bar was discovered about 30m to the west of the site. It had a small wooden 'haft' fitted within its socket and it lay at an angle as if having been thrown from the north. Currency bars are difficult to date but it probably belongs in the second or first centuries BC, a period in which offerings were not made along the causeway. Construction of a temporary conservation tank for the second logboat about 20m north of the bar's findspot revealed a timber post which may conceivably form part of a second, shorter causeway from which the currency bar and other Late Iron Age artefacts may have been deposited.

Discussion

The recovery of two log boats in the 2001 excavation would seem to imply that this lower, southern section of the causeway lay adjacent to a contemporary channel of the river Witham. Additionally, the more complex form of the third, or western row of posts may also indicate that the causeway was nearing its end. This proposal gains some support from a recent archaeological evaluation undertaken immediately to the south of the river (Allen 2002). This investigation failed to detect any evidence for a continuation of the causeway, but did determine that a large sandbank occupied the area of its projected alignment. As a consequence of these discoveries it is necessary to question whether it was actually a 'causeway' linking opposite sides of the river. Was it indeed a raised track across wet ground, or was it a jetty connecting dry land with navigable water? Or did it lead not to the river but to a freshwater pool within the river's floodplain? It is hoped that the post-excavation analysis, and particularly the environmental assessment, will provide further insight.

Most of the datable Iron Age finds date to the fourth and third centuries BC, at the end of or after the period in which the causeway was being maintained and rebuilt. Only three of the swords can be dated to the period of post row construction. The weapons and tools had distinctly different distributions, the swords and spears being dropped beneath or close to the causeway and most of the tools being deposited about 5m to the east of the causeway. This spatial patterning must reflect depositional choice and not post-depositional movement but it is not clear whether it indicates different moments of deposition or explicit choice of depositional placing for different categories of artefact in relation to the causeway, or both.

The élite nature of much of the British Iron Age metalwork from riverine and other watery contexts has been clearly recognised (Fitzpatrick 1984; Bradley 1990). This is evident at Fiskerton with the coral-inlaid sword in particular and the several pieces with curvilinear La Tène-style decoration. The many artefacts which are unique or are worked in unique ways, such as the figure-of-eight piece and the internally-fluted amber beads, similarly point to the unusual status of many of these objects. Although there is a dearth of contemporary Iron Age material from either settlements or burials in Lincolnshire, comparison can be drawn with those of east Yorkshire, 60 miles to the north. It is clear that there is a category of élite metalwork, particularly that with La Tène-style decoration from cemeteries such as Garton Station, Kirkburn, Danes Graves, Garton Slack and Wetwang Slack and that it occurs in burials which can be classified as among those of a social élite (Dent 1985; Stead 1985). More broadly, commentators have remarked that examples of Celtic art are associated with aristocratic wealth and that makers of such material also had distinctive status in Early Iron Age society.

The British contribution to La Tène art has been described as second to none, with about 35% of it coming from rivers and watery deposits (Stead 1996). The quality of some of the finds from the Witham is exceptional in European terms and, like the finds from the Thames and from the east Yorkshire burials, indicates a remarkable power base through which this material was accumulated, manufactured and dumped. The presence of exceptional masterpieces of martial art in the Witham points to a highly stratified society whose principal symbols related to warfare.

The International Significance Of Fiskerton

The 1981 and 2001 excavations on the Fiskerton causeway provide a rare context for the remarkable finds of Iron Age weaponry and tools in association with a wooden causeway. The Roman offerings are also unusual because they differ from the items normally recovered from dryland shrines, sanctuaries and temples. Even though we still know very little about it - where it went, whether it was associated with a settlement, where it sat within the prehistoric landscape - the Fiskerton causeway has provided a glimpse of prehistoric religious practices of votive deposition and many other aspects of prehistoric life which rarely survive.

Fiskerton is not the only special site of this kind but there are four reasons why it is more important than all of the other river deposition sites that are known in Europe:

1. It is well preserved, having been damaged only by canalisation of the river and by dewatering. Other comparable sites in the Thames and European rivers have been seriously damaged by dredging.

2. Even though just a small part of it has been excavated, it is potentially a remarkably large and rich Iron Age assemblage, equivalent to La Tène and Llyn Cerrig Bach in terms of the quality and quantity of metalwork and La Tène art.

3. Whereas some of the more important sites, such as the Bronze Age timber alignment at Flag Fen (Pryor 2001), appear to be broadly single-period deposits, the Fiskerton causeway is part of a sequence of prehistoric and historical period sites not only within the Fiskerton/Washingborough locality but also along this 20-mile stretch of the Witham.

4. Analysis of the causeway's felling dates has shown the potential importance of midwinter lunar total eclipse prediction in the 1st millennium BC (Chamberlain in press).

Fiskerton In Its Local Setting From The Neolithic To The Medieval Period

The chance finds recovered along the Witham valley between Lincoln and Tattershall in the last 250 years (Banks 1893; 1896; Davey 1973; White 1979a-d; Field and Parker Pearson in press) make it likely that Fiskerton is just one of a large number of votive deposition sites along this 20-mile stretch of river. It appears to have been just one of many causeways or deposition places of different dates from the Bronze Age to the Late Medieval period in the two parishes of Fiskerton and Washingborough. The Barlings-Bardney area is similarly important because of its likely votive deposits of different periods but also because it may preserve the physical relationships between votive sites and Christian religious houses. Thirdly, there may be as many as ten causeways (or causeway complexes) across the Witham or its edges in this stretch between Lincoln and Tattershall (see Everson and Stocker Fig.1, this volume).

- Studies of Iron Age wood technology and woodland management were only partial during the 1981 excavation and were hampered by the small size of the 2001 excavation. These aspects require more detailed work with fresh material.

- Environmental analyses (soil, beetles, pollen, macrofossils, diatoms, flies, soil micromorphology, geochemical analyses) were only partial in the 1981 excavation but will be more complete as a result of the 2001 excavation. Nevertheless, more work is required on environmental reconstruction at other points along the causeway's length.

- The extent of desiccation and plough damage to timbers and of corrosion to buried metal artefacts along the length of the causeway since 1981 is unknown but may be severe to the north of the 1981 and 2001 excavations. The extent and quality of their survival and preservation need to be assessed.

Other Likely Causeways And Offering Sites In The Fiskerton/Washingborough Area

A series of other locations may profit from excavation and survey to shed light on practices of votive deposition:

- The double post row south of the river in Washingborough parish is on a north-south alignment (along which Late Bronze Age socketed axes, an axe mould and other bronze artefacts have been found). This structure needs to be characterised, dated and localised in extent.

- The Washingborough Pumping Station site (Early Iron Age) needs further investigation, particularly along the length of the timber structure identified by the Washingborough Archaeology Group, to characterise it and define its extent. Votive deposition in Hallstatt periods B, C and D is very poorly understood and this may be one of the very few sites in Europe which can shed light on this phenomenon.

- The area adjacent to, and south of, Fiskerton churchyard has produced finds of Early and Middle Bronze Age stone tools and metalwork, hinting at votive deposition in this location at that date. Survey and test trenching might shed more light on this area's use in the Bronze Age.

- The locations of findspots for the Fiskerton Viking sword and the Anglo-Saxon triple brooch are known with reasonable precision and these areas may profit from survey and excavation to locate post-Roman votive deposition.

- The large rectilinear cropmarks at Cherry Willingham school and Branston have been tentatively identified as Roman sanctuary precincts comparable to those outside the *colonia* at Colchester. Trial excavation would enable this proposition to be evaluated.

- There are a number of other sites which would benefit from closer characterisation and assessment of potential (such as the Bronze Age barrow groups, the locations of Neolithic axe finds and, although unconnected with votive deposition, the Middle Palaeolithic handaxe findspot).

- The Late Iron Age currency bar found about 30m west of the Fiskerton causeway in 2001 may have been deposited on the southern edge of another votive deposition site, possibly in the area where an undated post was exposed in 2001 beneath the temporary wood conservation tank. This possibility needs to be explored.

Implementation

The Fiskerton-Washingborough component of the project should work as an integrated set of individual sub-projects which are separate yet contribute information and expertise amongst each other and share in the overall aims of the project. This component can be divided into three sub-projects:

1. Fiskerton causeway – geophysical, geochemical and remote-sensing surveys and excavation of the Iron Age causeway and deposits.

2. Fiskerton environs – survey and trial excavation of other potential causeways, deposition sites and selected round barrows in the vicinity.

3. Roman religious sites – survey and trial excavation of the cropmarks of the possible sanctuary sites.

Bibliography

Allen, M., 2002, *Proposed Flood Defence Improvement in Washingborough Parish,*

Lincolnshire (Unpublished Archaeological Evaluation Report, Lincoln, Pre-Construct Archaeology).

Banks, J., 1893, (c. 1800), 'An account of some ancient arms and utensils found in Lincolnshire, chiefly in the bed of the River Witham, between Kirkstead and Lincoln, when it was scoured out in 1787 and 1788', (ed anonymously) *Lincolnshire Notes and Queries*, 3, 196-201, 232-36.

Banks, J., 1896, (c. 1800). 'An account of some ancient arms and utensils found in Lincolnshire, chiefly in the bed of the River Witham, between Kirkstead and Lincoln, when it was scoured out in 1787 and 1788', (ed anonymously) *Lincolnshire Notes and Queries*, 4, 20-21, 61-62, 124-27.

Bradley, R., 1990, *The Passage of Arms: an archaeological analysis of prehistoric hoard and votive deposits* (Cambridge, Cambridge University Press).

Brunaux, J.-L., 1988, *The Celtic Gauls: Gods, Rites and Sanctuaries* (London, Seaby).

Brunaux, J.-L., Meniel, P. and Rapin, A. 1980, 'Un sanctuaire gaulois à Gournay-sur-Aronde (oise)', *Gallia*, 38, 1-25.

Chamberlain, A., in press, 'Saros cycles, lunar eclipses and the construction of the causeway' in Field, N. and Parker Pearson, M., *Fiskerton: An Iron Age Timber Causeway With Iron Age And Roman Votive Offerings. The 1981 Excavations* (Oxford, Oxbow).

Davey, P.J., 1973, 'Bronze Age metalwork from Lincolnshire', *Archaeologia*, 104, 51-127.

Dent, J.S., 1985, 'Three cart burials from Wetwang, Yorkshire', *Antiquity*, 59, 85-92.

Derks, T., 1998, *Gods, Temples and Ritual Practices: the transformation of religious ideas and values in Roman Gaul* (Amsterdam, Amsterdam University Press).

Duval, A., 1990, 'Quelques aspects du mobilier metallique en fer anciennement recueilli à Tronoën, en Saint-Jean-Trolimon (Finistère)', in Duval, A., Le Bihan, J.-P. and Menez, Y. (eds), *Les Gaulois d'Armorique. La fin de l'Age du Fer en Europe tempérée. Actes du XIIe colloque de l'AFEAF. Quimper. Mai 1988*, 23-45. Rennes: Revue Archéologique de l'Ouest, supplément no. 3.

Field, N. and Parker Pearson, M., in press, *Fiskerton: An Iron Age Timber Causeway With Iron Age And Roman Votive Offerings. The 1981 Excavations* (Oxford, Oxbow).

Fitzpatrick, A.P., 1984, 'The deposition of La Tène Iron Age metalwork in watery contexts in southern England', in Cunliffe, B. and Miles, D. (eds), *Aspects of the Iron Age in Central Southern Britain*, University of Oxford Committee for Archaeology, 2, 178-90 (Oxford).

Fitzpatrick, A.P., 1996, 'Night and day: the symbolism of astral signs on later Iron Age anthropomorphic short swords', *Proceedings of the Prehistoric Society*, 62, 373-98.

Fox, C., 1947, *A Find of the Early Iron Age from Llyn Cerrig Bach, Anglesey* (Cardiff, National Museum of Wales).

Hillam, J., 1992, 'Dendrochronology in England: the dating of a wooden causeway from Lincolnshire and a logboat from Humberside'. *Actes du XIIIe Colloque de l'A.F.E.A.F. Le Berry et le Limousin à l'Age du Fer. Artisanat du bois et des matières organiques*. Limousin: Association pour la Recherche Archéologique en Limousin. 137-141.

Hunter, F., 2001, 'The carnyx in Iron Age Europe', *Antiquaries Journal*, 81, 77-108.

Ilkjaer, J. and Lønstrup, J., 1982, 'Interpretation of the great votive deposits of Iron Age weapons', *Journal of Danish Archaeology*, 1, 95-103.

Olsen, S., in press, 'The bone and antler artefacts: their manufacture and use', in Field, N. and Parker Pearson, M., *Fiskerton: An Iron Age Timber Causeway With Iron Age And Roman Votive Offerings. The 1981 Excavations* (Oxford, Oxbow).

Pearson, G., 1796, 'Observations on some ancient metallic arms and utensils with experiments to determine their composition', *Philosophical Transactions of the Royal Society of London*, 86, 395-451.

Piggott, S., 1959, 'The Carnyx in Early Iron Age Britain', *Antiquaries Journal*, 39, 19-32.

Pryor, F., 2001, *Archaeology and Environment of the Flag Fen Basin* (London, English Heritage).

Randsborg, K., 1995, *Hjortspring: Warfare and Sacrifice in Early Europe*, (Aarhus, Aarhus University Press).

Rosenberg, G., 1937, 'Hjortspringfundet', *Nordiske Fortidsminder*, 3 (1) (Copenhagen, Gyldendal).

Schwab, H., 1989, *Archéologie de la 2e Correction des Eax du Jura. Vol. 1 - Les Celtes sur la Broye et la Thielle* (Fribourg, Editions Universitaires Fribourg Suisse).

Stead, I.M., 1979, *The Arras Culture* (York, Yorkshire Philosophical Society).

Stead, I.M., 1985, *The Battersea Shield* (London, British Museum).

Stead, I.M., 1996, *Celtic Art in Britain Before the Roman Conquest*, 2nd edition (London, British Museum).

Stead, I.M., in press, 'The Iron Age military artefacts', in Field, N. and Parker Pearson, M., *Fiskerton: An Iron Age Timber Causeway With Iron Age And Roman Votive Offerings. The 1981 Excavations* (Oxford, Oxbow).

Vouga, P., 1923, *La Tène; monographie de la station* (Leipzig, Hiersmann).

Wait, G.A., 1985, *Ritual and Religion in Iron Age Britain*, British Archaeological Reports (British Series), 149.

White, A.J., 1979a, *Dug-out Boats from Lincolnshire and South Humberside*, Lincolnshire Museums Information Sheet, Archaeology Series 3 (Lincoln).

White, A.J., 1979b, *Antiquities from the River Witham, Part 1, Prehistoric and Roman*, Lincolnshire Museums Information Sheet, Archaeology Series 12 (Lincoln).

White, A.J., 1979c, *Antiquities from the River Witham, Part 2, Anglo-Saxon and Viking*, Lincolnshire Museums Information Sheet, Archaeology Series 13 (Lincoln).

White, A.J., 1979d, *Antiquities from the River Witham, Part 3, Mediaeval*, Lincolnshire Museums Information Sheet, Archaeology Series 14 (Lincoln).

PALAEOENVIRONMENTAL RESEARCH DESIGN FOR THE WITHAM VALLEY

by Charly French and James Rackham

Introduction

The c. 35km length of the Witham valley between the city of Lincoln and Tattershall remains one of the last interface zones of fenland and river valley landscape to be subject to intensive archaeological and palaeoenvironmental investigation in the fenland region of eastern England. Nonetheless, a combination of several research and contract driven archaeological excavations and landscape projects has already made available a large amount of archaeological and palaeoenvironmental data, but this has neither been integrated nor complemented by new data to produce a well dated series of Holocene landscape sequences for the area.

For the last four years we have been collecting data and samples from the valley as a prelude to producing a proposal for a multidisciplinary project. To date most of this work has been developer funded and is based largely upon the results of commercial geotechnical investigations, with access on some projects to the core samples taken during these investigations. As yet the level of analysis has been limited and few radiocarbon dates have been obtained although some sampling of continuous cores for detailed palaeo-environmental analysis has been possible with funded study in progress on one site.

The primary objectives of this project would be to map the maximum coastline; establish the sea level changes in the valley over the last few thousand years; model the topography and landscape and produce a series of time dimension palaeo-environmental reconstructions of the valley and its limestone hinterland. We believe the results should be closely tied into the archaeological exploitation of the valley in prehistoric and historic times and used to assess the further archaeological potential of the area and inform on the needs for management of the resource.

The Environmental Context

There are four major landscape zones in the proposed study area: fenland, floodplain, terraces and limestone hinterland, although in the past saltmarsh and estuarine landscapes were also present. Preservation environments in these zones will vary greatly from deeply buried and waterlogged, to damp margins, and to dry and plough truncated higher ground. All of these undoubtedly inter-relate, and the task is to elucidate differences and inter-relationships between the archaeological and the palaeoenvironmental record in each zone.

The valley floor immediately east of Lincoln is narrow, about 1km wide. It widens out quite quickly and 4km east at Fiskerton the valley has widened to over 2km where it turns south-east, continuing to widen until at Bardney it is 6.5km wide (Fig. 1). Over the next 15km the valley sides remain broadly parallel before opening out into South Kyme, Wildmore and West Fens below the confluence of the rivers Bain and Slea at Dogdyke. Upstream the valley widens immediately west of Lincoln where the rivers Witham and Till (now the present day Fossdyke) join and have formed the Brayford Pool a water body of very considerable antiquity. 1.5km south-west of the Brayford a second large ancient water body, the Swan Pool, occupies part of the valley floor.

Brief Review Of Current Information

The valley at Lincoln which cuts through the Lincolnshire limestone ridge, with underlying lower Lias clays to the west, and the overlying upper Jurassic clays to the east, is filled with fluvio-glacial sands and gravels and Holocene freshwater and marine sediments. The river, presently canalised along much of its length below Lincoln, hugs the north side of the valley floor from Fiskerton downstream, a course it is believed to have occupied since at least the eleventh century (Lane 1993). The depth of the post-glacial sediments infilling the valley between Lincoln and Tattershall reach a maximum of about 10m. The eastern end of this stretch is largely filled with marine sediments laid down on the valley floor during periods of lower sea level. The Lincoln end and the valley margins are filled with sands, clays, organic silts and peats (Waller 1994). Much of these latter deposits may cover earlier land surfaces which were inundated by sea and freshwater as a result of sea level and other hydrological changes during the post-glacial period. Waller (1994) has suggested

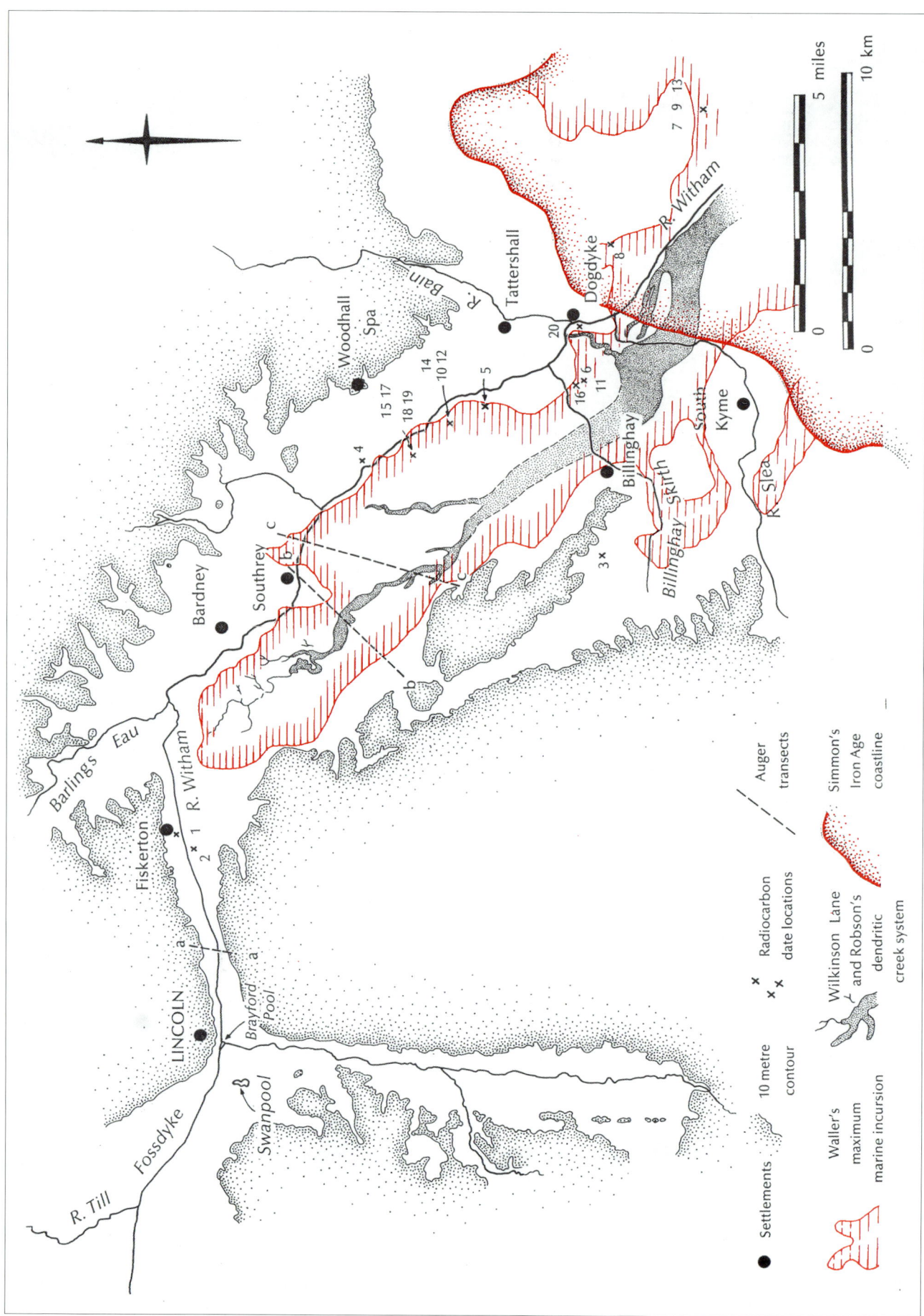

Figure 1 The Witham Valley, showing the approximate limits of marine sedimentation and ancient creek systems with the locations of auger transects and radiocarbon dating samples (in Table 1). Drawn by D.W. Hopkins

that the marine sedimentation progressed as far up the valley as Branston Fen, just south of Short Ferry, between 3700 and 3300 BP (see Fig. 1) but sediments observed in cores taken at Fiskerton (unpublished) have shown the presence of laminated inter-tidal deposits suggesting that marine sedimentation approached even further up the valley floor. The absence of such sediments in the boreholes for the Eastern Bypass (see Figs. 1 and 2) suggests that the narrowness and energy regime of the river at this point were unsuitable for the deposition of the laminated sediments so characteristic of the broad flat areas of the fenlands. This does not mean that the river was not tidal at this point. The occurrence of fine laminated silts, typical of fenland sediments, in deposits within the Brayford Pool may indicate that there were periods when the Brayford was also tidal. Wilkinson (1987) records brackish water elements among the diatoms in Roman and medieval deposits in the Brayford and 'fen clays' which suggests perhaps some tidal influence in historic times.

Downstream, Wilkinson (1987) has plotted the main elements of an estuarine creek system, recognised from soil mapping (Robson et al 1974) and aerial photographs, that runs through the middle of the valley (see Fig. 1), and a large area of peat south and east of Fiskerton. The highly dendritic pattern of this creek system is clearly visible in the aerial photograph of Nocton Fen illustrated in the Soil Survey volume for Woodhall Spa (Robson et al 1974). Further downstream, Lane (1993) identified a stretch of very large creek west and south of Dogdyke (see Fig. 1) which he considered to represent a prehistoric course of the river Witham. This is likely to be a continuation of the creek system identified upstream which infilled with silts and sands as the estuarine waters retreated from the valley. Lane (op cit) has suggested that this channel may have continued to function through the Roman period.

Waller's (1994) landscape model for the Witham shows the progressive retreat of the sea from the valley during later prehistory, with the development of extensive peats on the valley floor. Simmons (1980, 2001) has proposed that the Iron Age coastline lay only just beyond the opening out of the valley at the point where the Slea meets the Witham (see Fig. 1) with the Roman coastline only a little further east. There are slight discrepancies between Simmon's coastline and that suggested by Waller's model for the end of the Iron Age and Roman period. The latter proposes that the coastline extends into the Witham valley, but that it does not approach quite so far inland, where the valley opens out onto the fen. Such discrepancies are not unexpected and it should be remembered that both models are subject to limited data and were not designed to be applied to such a small geographic area as this region of the Witham valley. Finally, during the post-Roman and medieval periods, the model suggests that the marine sedimentation had ceased completely in the valley and the valley floor was largely covered by developing peats. Lane (op cit) has suggested that the present course of the river had been established by the time of Domesday. Nevertheless, his description of the upper clay and fine sediment fills of the prehistoric course in Hart's Grounds and Pelham's Lands (Lane 1993, 17-19) suggests that this channel was no longer functioning as the main river outlet when these sediments were deposited. The present river course must, therefore, already have been cut, although any attempt at ascertaining when this occurred would be speculative.

The existing extent of the surface peats is illustrated for the central part of the valley by the Soil Survey (Robson et al 1974). This is much diminished from earlier reports such as Clarke in 1848, the late nineteenth century Geological Survey map, Wheeler's map of 1868 and Skertchly's map of 1877 where he records a thickness of peat within the Witham valley of between six and eight feet. The Witham Fens underwent their first major drainage between 1777 and 1797 (Robinson 2001) when 25,000 acres were drained, while large areas of the East, West and Wildmore Fens downstream were drained in 1801-14. Little of the peat build up during the post-Roman and medieval periods is likely to have survived these and more recent drainage and agricultural activity, but deposits may survive beneath embankments, roads and river banks.

The degradation of peats associated with this drainage and agricultural activity is continuing and increasing exposures of the barrow fields and structures such as the Fiskerton causeway are testament to the loss of these later sediments. J.D. Robson has suggested that peat was still forming in the valley up until the time of enclosure and that as much as two metres may have been lost (pers comm. in Field and Parker Pearson in press) in some areas of the valley.

Recent Surveys

Four borehole transects across the valley have recently been undertaken in advance of the laying of gas pipelines and of a proposed new eastern

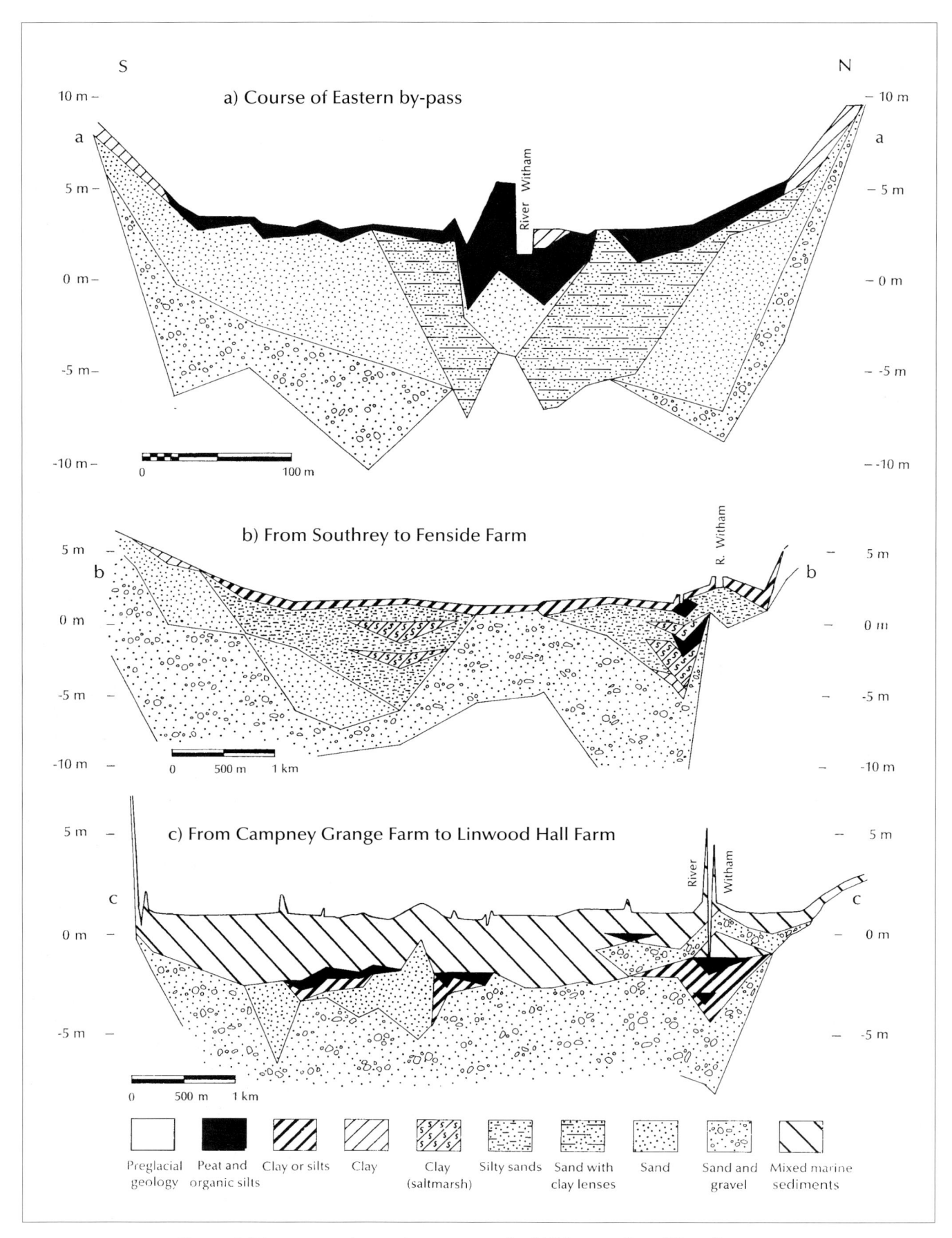

Figure 2 Diagrammatic sections across the Witham valley fill sediments.
(see figure 1 for the location of the auger transects). Drawn by D.W. Hopkins

bypass for Lincoln (Fig. 1). One of these was undertaken over two decades ago and the data has not been located although an unpublished assessment of the deposits was undertaken by J. M. Monaghan. Assessment of the bore logs for the other three transects was possible and diagrammatic reconstructions of the valley sediments have been produced from the data available in the engineers' logs (Fig. 2). It should be noted that such logs are subject to generalisations and errors in sediment description and the reconstructions should be viewed with some caution. Until new boreholes with detailed sedimentological descriptions are undertaken the conclusions must remain provisional.

Just east of Lincoln the Holocene sediments appear to infill the north central part of the valley floor (Fig. 2a). The post-glacial channel appears to have scoured out all the fluvio-glacial sands and gravels and is floored by the upper Jurassic clays. A sequence of fine and coarse grey sands with organics and shells is overlain by up to 3.5m of peat and organic silts, capped immediately adjacent to the river by alluvial clays.

Downstream, between Southrey and Fenside Farm, two post-glacial channels are present in the reconstructed section (Fig. 2b). In contrast to the section immediately east of Lincoln the bulk of the sediments in this section are marine sands and silts with episodes of what are at present interpreted as saltmarsh clay silts. The lack of any identifiably freshwater sediments in the logs for the lower deposits in the southern channel perhaps suggests that this was largely a tidal channel draining the river estuary and tidal flats and, presumably having filled, ceased to have any major role during the freshwater phase. In contrast the sedimentary sequence in the northern channel suggests a change from marine to freshwater, back to marine and finally back to freshwater conditions. The latest episode producing alluvial clay/silt and peat deposits across much of the valley floor, although the latter appear to have been largely degraded and removed as a result of land drainage and agricultural activity.

Finally, the third transect crossed the valley between Linwood Hall and Campney Grange Farm (Fig. 2c). The two main drainage channels recognised in the Southrey section are still apparent in this one although there is a possibility that a third more southerly channel may also have existed. In contrast to the borehole logs for the Southrey transect these reveal peat and organic silty clays of freshwater origin on the north and south side of the valley associated with both the main estuarine channels. Peat deposits in a number of boreholes on either side of the southern channel reflect a freshwater episode within the largely marine sediment sequence. The channel on the north side of the valley with its peat horizons and sandy gravel deposits suggests that the present day river still runs broadly on a course it has occupied for many centuries. The southern channel in both these latter sections may well correspond to the roddon identified by Robson (*op cit*) from the soil survey and plotted on Fig. 1.

No upper peats were recorded in any of the boreholes for this eastern section and they have presumably been lost or exist only in the topsoil.

Unfortunately none of these data are tied to a chronological framework, and apart from the Eastern Bypass and Southrey transect where samples and cores from the geotechnical work have been retained against future funding of radiocarbon dating and post-excavation analysis, we can expect to get no further information than that available from the borehole logs. A few deposits in this part of the valley have been radiocarbon dated (Table 1) and afford the beginnings of a chronology for some of the sediments but we cannot reliably link these dates to the sequences we have illustrated. The radiocarbon dates for the lower peats sampled along the edges of the valley and downstream at Woodhall Spa, Gipsey Bridge and Bettinsons Bridge between 0 and –1.7m OD have given dates reflecting the build up of these sediments between 2000 and 3000 BC indicating that the freshwater phase and peat formation represented by the peats in the Campney Grange Farm and Southrey transects at similar and slightly lower levels OD may be equatable with the late Neolithic and early Bronze Age. This represents the period after a major phase of inland marine transgression and just before the maximum inland extension of the sea suggested by the model developed from the detailed work on the Fenland Survey and sea level change programme (Waller 1994) and indicated in Fig. 1. The only archaeological dates for this area are: a Bronze Age date from a burnt mound at Stixwould (Snelling and Gale 2001) on the northern edge of the valley which was covered with peats and alluvial sediments and beyond the limits of marine sedimentation; wood near the base of a peat overlying a barrow at Walcott Common dated to the early first millennium BC; a post from Washingborough; and a middle to late Iron Age peat layer overlying a buried sandy soil with Bronze Age flints on the northern edge of the valley at

No. on Fig 1	Lab No.	Site	Material	C14 measure	Approx. Height OD	Calibrated date at 95% confidence
1	Beta-125858	Fiskerton	peat	2140±60	4.0m OD	BC 330-320 & 205-60 BC
2	Q-1163	Washingborough Fen	*Betula* post	2253±80	-	BC 640-170
3	Har-3362	Walcott Common	Wood	2540±100	Near base of basal peat overlying a barrow	BC 910-400
4	Beta-161060	Stixwould	Charcoal	3570±70	Between 0.25 & 0.75m OD - burnt mound	BC 2130-2080 & 2060-1730
5	Har-149	Woodhall Spa	Base of basal peat	3620±130	approx 0m OD	BC 2385-1685
6	Har-148	Woodhall Spa	Base of basal peat	3770±130	approx -1.25m OD	BC 2540-1810
7	Q-2567	Gipsey Bridge	Transgressive contact of basal peat	3790±80	-0.48 to -0.52m OD	BC 2470-1985
8	Q-2568	Bettinsons Bridge	Transgressive contact of basal peat	3810±50	-0.22 to -0.26m OD	BC 2470-2045
9	Q-2565	Gipsey Bridge	Transgressive contact of basal peat	3825±75	-0.12 to -0.16m OD	BC 2490-2045
10	IGS-109	Woodhall Spa	Transgressive contact of basal peat	3945±100	-1.45m OD	BC 2845-2140
11	Har-189	Woodhall Spa	Base of basal peat	3950±120	-1.25m OD	BC 2865-2130
12	IGS-111	Woodhall Spa	Base of basal peat	3980±100	-0.09m OD	BC 2860-2190
13	Q-2566	Gipsey Bridge	Base of basal peat	4070±80	-0.5 to -0.54m OD	BC 2895-2455
14	Har-147	Woodhall Spa	Base of basal peat	4080±130	-0.9m OD	BC 2925-2290
15	Har-151	Woodhall Spa	Base of basal peat	4120±130	-0.9m OD	BC 2945-2345
16	IGS-112	Woodhall Spa	Base of basal peat	4130±100	-1.25m OD	BC 2925-2460
17	IGS-110	Woodhall Spa	Base of basal peat	4155±100	-1.7m OD	BC 2930-2475
18	Har-150	Woodhall Spa	Transgressive contact of basal peat	4160±130	-1.45m OD	BC 3040-2455
19	Har-192	Woodhall Spa	Base of basal peat	4210±120	-1.7m OD	BC 3030-2500
20	Birm-447	Tattershall	*Pinus*	4570±150	-	BC 3691-2910

Table 1 Radiocarbon dates from the Witham Valley below Lincoln.

Fiskerton (see also Field, Parker Pearson and Rylatt, this volume).

Apart from the Stixwould date, which suggests that the 'burnt mound' was functioning during this period of peat build up, the archaeological dates are all first millennium BC as is the dendrochronologically dated causeway at Fiskerton (Field, Parker Pearson and Rylatt, this volume). Surviving waterlogged material of earlier periods of activity is presumably buried more deeply beneath the alluvial, peat and marine sediments than investigations have so far managed to reveal. The increasingly visible barrows in the Washingborough and Stainfield groups (Everson and Hayes, 1984) suggest that some of this earlier activity is likely to become visible over future years as agricultural activity and drainage continues to erode the existing ground surface. A probable buried soil horizon, underlying laminated intertidal sediments, observed in coring over two metres beneath the Fiskerton causeway suggests that Mesolithic and Neolithic ground surfaces and any associated archaeology may have survived the erosion associated with rising sea level, at least within some areas in the valley.

The Brayford Pool

Immediately upstream of Lincoln at the confluence of the old river Till and the river Witham is the Brayford Pool (see Fig. 1). This pool has been much larger in the past, and assessment of the geotechnical data on the Lincoln University site has identified extensive depths of peat around the existing pool, plus what appears to be the original course of the river Till and a high spot or promontory of sand between the two rivers (Fig. 3). Investigations north of the pool at Brayford North (LBN00) have identified extensive peat and waterlain sediments also under the north bank and the pool may once have approached almost as far north as Newland in this area. Several radiocarbon dates have now been obtained from the organic horizons in the sequence at locations around the Brayford (Table 2) and indicate organic sediments that span from the Mesolithic to the medieval period and afford an exceptional opportunity to study the palaeoenvironmental history of Lincoln and its immediate surroundings, and the development of the Brayford and its changes in level and condition. Characteristics of the sequence in the Brayford may well reflect patterns of change to the river system downstream and indicate periods of control, or loss of it, of the water flow and levels, and the impact of changes in sea level.

With this short summary of some of the palaeoenvironmental data available for the Witham we can now review the objectives of the project.

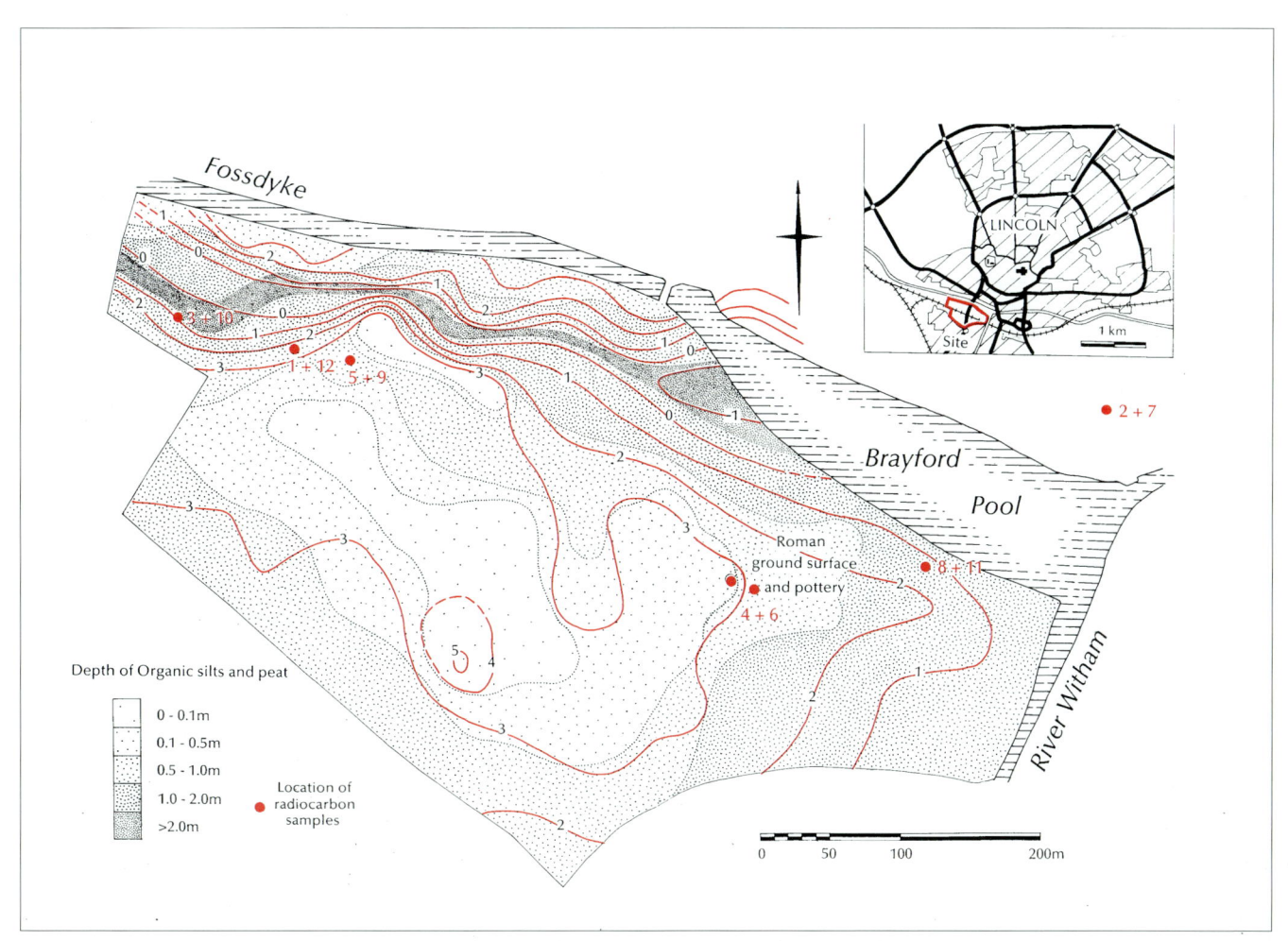

Figure 3 Lincoln University Site: Contour plot of the upper surface of natural sands (in red) with the extent and depth of organic sediments. The locations of radiocarbon dating samples (in Table 2) are shown.
Drawn by D.W. Hopkins

No.	Lab No.	Site		material	C14 measure	Approx. Height OD	Calibrated date at 95% confidence
1	Beta-155289	Lincoln Univ. Ph. 3	BH2	Peat	730±60	2.7m	AD 1200 - 1320 and AD 1350 - 1390
2	Beta-157533	Brayford North	BH2	Peat	1260±60	2.22-2.32m	AD 660 to 900
3	Beta-155291	Lincoln Univ. Ph. 3	BH3	Peat	1270±60	3.03m	AD 650 - 890
4	Beta-171900	Lincoln Univ. Ph. 6	TT1	Peat	1960±60	3.03m3.08	BC 80 – AD 150
5	Beta-155287	Lincoln Univ. Ph. 3	BH1	Peat	1980±40	2.6m	BC 50 - AD 100
6	Beta-171899	Lincoln Univ. Ph. 6	TT1	Wood	2920±40	2.33-2.38	BC 1200 - 940
7	Beta-157534	Brayford North	BH2	Peat	3020±60	0.85-0.95m	BC 1410 to 1060
8	-	Lincoln Univ. Eval.	TP 33	Peat	3100±60	Between 2.14 and 4.14m	BC 1515-1223
9	Beta-155288	Lincoln Univ. Ph. 3	BH1	Peat	3170±40	1.57m	BC 1520 - 1390
10	Beta-155292	Lincoln Univ. Ph. 3	BH3	Peat	4650±100	0.88m	BC 3650 –3090
11	-	Lincoln Univ. Eval.	TP 33	Peat	4800±50	Between 1.74-2.14m	BC 3698 - 3382
12	Beta-155290	Lincoln Univ. Ph. 3	BH2	Peat	7420±40	0.7m OD	BC 6390 - 6220

* the numbers refer to the locations marked in Fig. 3

Table 2 Radiocarbon dates from the Brayford Pool, Lincoln arranged in chronological order.

Objectives

The objectives of the new project range from the site specific to more broadly based landscape change issues. At the site level, it is essential initially to understand Fiskerton's later prehistoric landscape setting and sequence before moving on to the other ten, possibly similar, post-alignments downstream in the study area. These site locations will act as excellent *foci* for transects for the associated landscape investigation. The body of data already collected from the Brayford Pool afford an excellent opportunity to study changes in this important water body, the date of construction of the Fossdyke, and the prehistoric and historic changes to the immediate environs of Lincoln.

At the wider scale, it is essential to elucidate the sequence of palaeochannels downstream of Lincoln and their associated floodplains. Chronological and vegetational sequences will need to be established to chart the Holocene development of the river valley. In addition, deposit mapping will be necessary to assess the probable land-use and preservation zones in the valley system through time and the sequence and timing of the major marine phases.

Using site specific and transect derived sampling intervals, new pedological and palaeo-vegetational data will be marshalled with which to construct detailed sequences of landscape change in the valley, and to chart the effects of human activities, sea level change and other factors on the river valley system and associated hinterland.

Methodological Approach

A variety of scales of approach will be necessary, as follows:

- to correlate all existing commercial information already obtained from recent developer-funded projects

- to collate all existing borehole data for the valley including that generated by the Environmental

Agency in connection with their flood relief works in the valley

- to map the study area using the aerial photographic record, particularly to prospect for the dendritic creek systems of the inter-tidal zone, palaeochannels, buried floodplain and fenland deposit zones

- to use the existing post-alignment sites as the central points for a series of landscape transects across the river valley; these transects will first involve augering at 100m or 200m intervals to construct valley cross-sectional maps, and prospect for buried soils and waterlogged deposits

- prospect for later Roman and medieval sequences by specifically targeting embankments, raised roads and river banks in the auger survey

- on the basis of these datasets, target a series of the best preserved areas on- and off- site for sample trenching to obtain palaeoenvironmental datasets and radiocarbon samples

- laboratory analyses of these datasets, associated with a full dating programme

- production of palaeoenvironmental sequence histories and terrain sequence maps of the study area, including revision of the model on marine sedimentation and its chronology

- production of a predictive model for the potential distribution of archaeological sites beneath the alluvial and marine sediments and their potential quality of survival

- re-evaluation of the extent of the loss of deposits from the floor of the valley to inform the debate on the management of the archaeological resource

In addition, the present day hydrological regime will require investigation in order to address the problem of long-term preservation of the later prehistoric post-alignment sites in the study area. This is probably best tackled by the setting up of a separate research project with English Heritage backing to investigate on-site conditions of preservation and for long-term monitoring.

Funding

Several funding combinations may be avenues to explore. There has already been some developer-funded input in terms of providing borehole sequencing and radiometric data for the upper part of the study area. A variety of external funding bodies should be approached such as the British Academy, the Arts and Humanities Research Board, the Leverhulme Trust, the McDonald Institute for Archaeological Research and English Heritage. In particular, if seed funding could be found from English Heritage and the McDonald Institute in order to correlate all existing data, write a new integrated research design and conduct preliminary assessment-type fieldwork, this would be one of the best ways of starting the new research project. The Brayford Pool could be approached as a second, perhaps separate, project with more localised objectives and a strong historical element to give a landscape context for the Roman, Saxon and medieval town. Then a much larger application could be made say to the Leverhulme Trust, bringing in all associated projects within the Witham Valley Project.

Bibliography

Carrot, J., Hall, A., Issitt, M., Lancaster, S., Kenward, H. and Milles, A., 1994, 'Evaluation of biological remains from deposits at the University for Lincolnshire site, Brayford, Lincoln (Site code UCL94)', EAU report 94/21 in Wragg.

Chowne, P., 1980, 'Bronze Age settlement in South Lincolnshire', in Barrett, J. and Bradley R. (eds), *The British Later Bronze Age*. BAR BS83 (ii), 265-305.

Clarke, A., 1848, 'On the Great Level of the fens including the Fens of South Lincolnshire', *Journal Royal Agric. Soc.* 8, 80-133.

Everson, P. and Hayes, T., 1984, 'Lincolnshire from the air', in Field N. and White, A. (eds), *A Prospect of Lincolnshire, being collected articles on the history and traditions of Lincolnshire in honour of Ethel H. Rudkin* (Lincoln).

Field, N., 1986, 'An Iron Age timber causeway at Fiskerton, Lincolnshire', *Fenland Research* 3, 49-53.

Field, N. and Parker Pearson, M., in press, *Fiskerton: An Iron Age Timber Causeway With Iron Age*

And Roman Votive Offerings. The 1981 Excavations (Oxford, Oxbow).

Lane, T.W., 1993, *The Fenland Project Number 8: Lincolnshire Survey, the Northern Fen-Edge*, East Anglian Archaeology 66.

Rackham, D.J., 1997, *Proposed Hatton to Silk Willoughby Gas Pipeline; Palaeoenvironmental assessment of the Witham Valley stretch* (Unpublished report for Network Archaeology Ltd).

Rackham, D. J., 1998a, *Lincoln City Eastern By-Pass. Specification for the Palaeoenvironmental assessment of the Witham Valley stretch* (Unpublished report for the City of Lincoln Archaeological Unit).

Rackham, D.J., 1998b, *University of Lincolnshire, Brayford South, Lincoln: University Phase III Accommodation, Environmental assessment* (Unpublished report for the City of Lincoln Archaeological Unit)

Rackham, D.J., 1998c, *Brayford Wharf East 1998; Borehole investigation* (Unpublished report for the City of Lincoln Archaeological Unit).

Rackham, D.J., 1999, *Lincoln City Eastern By-Pass: Assessment of the archaeological and palaeoenvironmental potential of the sediments infilling the Witham Valley along the line of the proposed Lincoln City Eastern Bypass based upon borehole logs and samples* (Unpublished report for the City of Lincoln Archaeological Unit).

Rackham, D.J., 2000, *Hatton to Silk Willoughby natural gas Pipeline: Assessment of the recent deposits and archaeological potential of the route across the floor of the Witham Valley* (Unpublished report for Network Archaeology Ltd).

Robinson, D.N., 2001, 'Drainage and reclamation', pg 72-73 in Bennett, S. and Bennett, N., (eds) *An Historical Atlas of Lincolnshire* (Phillimore).

Robson, J.D., George, H. and Heaven, F. W., 1974, *Soils in Lincolnshire I, Sheet TF16.* Soil Survey Record No. 22 (Harpenden).

Shennan, I., 1994, 'The Flandrian Deposits - Chapter 14. North-Western Fens' in Waller 1994.

Simmons, B.B., 1980, 'Iron Age and Roman coasts around the Wash', in Thompson, F.H. (ed) *Archaeology and Coastal Change.* London: Society of Antiquaries Occasional Paper (new series) 1, 56-73.

Simmons, B.B., 2001, 'Iron Age and Roman Coasts around the Wash', pg 18-21 in Bennett, S. and Bennett, N. (eds) *An Historical Atlas of Lincolnshire* (Phillimore).

Snelling, A. and Gale, R., 2001, *Stixwould, Lincolnshire – STXG 01:Environmental Archaeology Report* (Unpublished report for PCA Lincoln).

Skertchly, S.B.J., 1877, *The Geology of the Fenland* (HMSO).

Valentine, K.W.G. and Dalrymple, J. B., 1975, 'The identification, lateral variation, and chronology of two buried palaeocatenas at Woodhall Spa and West Runton, England', *Quaternary Research* **5**, 551-90.

Waller, M.,1994, *The Fenland Project, No.9: Flandrian Environmental change in Fenland*, East Anglian Archaeology No. 70.

Wheeler, W.H., 1990, *A History of the Fens of South Lincolnshire*, reprint of 1868 edition, Paul Watkins, Stamford.

Wilkinson, T.J., 1987, 'Palaeoenvironments of the Upper Witham Fen: a preliminary view', *Fenland Research* 4, 52-56.

Wragg, K., 1994, *Site of Proposed University College of Lincolnshire, Brayford South, Lincoln; Archaeological recording*, CLAU Archaeological Report No. 106.

LOCAL AUTHORITY CULTURAL RESOURCE MANAGEMENT

Jim Bonnor and Steve Catney

Introduction

The discipline of Cultural Resource Management (CRM) includes the collection of data relating to the historic environment, its synthesis and interpretation, the modelling of the past, and the creation of appropriate research agendas for future work. Analysis of the data may result in a number of options presenting themselves, such as further data collection (to enhance the record or address gaps identified), interpretation and educational projects, or the implementation of management options, *e.g.* excavation. Since the launch (in Lincoln in 1990) of Planning Policy Guidance Note 16 (Archaeology & Planning) the resources available to the discipline of Cultural Resource Management have been artificially biased towards the development control process, however, the challenge to cultural resource managers remains that of effective management of the historic landscape with the limited financial and human resources currently available.

A number of organisations and individuals have a role in CRM both locally and nationally. This paper addresses some of the issues specifically as they are dealt with in Lincolnshire and particularly within local government. Whilst focussing on development control and the planning process and the challenges faced by cultural resource managers, I shall attempt a wider look at CRM in Lincolnshire, with a discussion of some of the specific issues and options that must be addressed as part of the Witham Valley Research Project.

Cultural Resource Management

Archaeological cultural resource management within Local Authorities covers a wide remit. Good CRM starts with the collection of data, which is processed, catalogued and utilised to create, and then enhance, the local Sites and Monuments Record (SMR). The SMR incorporates a wide range of data which traditionally includes aerial photographs, details from excavations and other archaeological activities and records of casual finds. However, with the development of relational databases and geographical information systems, more and more data can now be utilised within SMRs. Datasets which might now be incorporated include palaeoenvironmental data; specialist datasets from other partners (*e.g.* LIDAR - accurate topographic survey using an airborne laser); flood risk data from the Environment Agency; and information emanating from Countryside Stewardship Scheme applications to DEFRA.

The Lincolnshire Conservation Services Team is a multidisciplinary group ranging from archaeologists and built-heritage professionals, to ecologists, tree and woodland experts and managers of protected sites and landscapes. The SMR, with the archaeological record at its core, is now being expanded to create a County Environmental Record which will support all the professional interests of the team. Working within a Highways and Planning Directorate also means that the CRM professional has access to all of the data required for land use planning. It is only with such a detailed, locally managed set of data that meaningful cultural resource management decisions can be made and appropriate advice given.

SMRs/Environmental Records covering too small an area tend to be inadequately resourced and limit the ability to look at whole landscapes or put individual sites into their wider context. Conversely, records covering too large an area are not able to hold the detail required by cultural resource managers and are cumbersome to curate. In fact, the county system appears to provide an optimum geographical area for an SMR, however, an exception to this observation arises when creating a detailed record for the management of the archaeology of a large historic urban area, for example Lincoln City. Here, the detail of data required better lends itself to an Urban Archaeological Database (UAD) focussed on the urban area and its immediate environs. The ultimate national archaeological record system will be able to network SMRs and UADs seamlessly and to interrogate their combined data for any user defined area.

Once a comprehensive database has been created, the CRM process requires:

- interpretation (or more likely multiple interpretations) of the data
- response to consultations on issues that might affect the resource

- proactive management, identifying knowledge gaps and informing research proposals
- designation and protection of some sites, and the excavation of others
- education and outreach work.

In order to achieve effective CRM a number of partnerships are required both within local authorities (*e.g.* between development control staff, museums and education), between various tiers of local authority and between national and local organisations within the public and private sectors.

Cultural Resource Management can be split into three areas:

1) <u>Proactive work</u>: Excavations; survey; education; public liaison; recording finds; the production of research agendas; and so on. Although these are in many ways the most interesting and arguably the most important elements in the archaeological process, (and often the main reason most of us became archaeologists in the first place) very few of these activities are carried out by local authorities. The community archaeologists of the Heritage Trust of Lincolnshire do carry out a number of programmes of work with the community through their district councils. In addition, the Heritage Trust receive core funding from Lincolnshire County Council and carry out much good community liaison (see paper by D Start in this volume), publication and some research work.

Most of the archaeologists active in CRM undertake talks and presentations at all levels, to professional groups, developers and parish councils. Lincolnshire County Council has a small amount of funding available for an ongoing research excavation programme and has been working with Durham University on an annual basis. Detailed finds recording also takes place and a Finds Liaison Officer (FLO) will be in post by the time this paper is published. This post is part of a national initiative financed by Heritage Lottery and central government funding through the Department for Culture Media and Sport. The FLO will work in close partnership with the county museum service.

Whilst a lot of good proactive CRM is undertaken and the staff delivering these services work extremely hard (often carrying out much of the work in their own time) not enough is achieved in these areas at present.

2) <u>Reactive Management – by negotiation</u>: Consultations on issues where there is extremely limited or no statutory control *e.g.* for many agricultural activities. Some of the impact of these works can be influenced through pro-active and targeted work, particularly the promotion and implementation of agri-environment schemes. Such schemes are set to become increasingly important for the management of historic landscapes on farmed land, not least because major changes are afoot in the Common Agricultural Policy. For further comment on agri-environment schemes and legislation in general see Went (this volume). Presently, there are a large number of successful Countryside Stewardship Schemes (CSS) in Lincolnshire (approximately 100 per annum) many of which include a benefit to archaeology but, in general, payments to farmers are not based on conservation activities but on subsidised crop production. However, there is a gradual and perceptible change towards conservation in the countryside which has accelerated over the last few years, culminating in the Curry Report, the Rural White Paper and the Countryside and Rights of Way Act. These documents have examined the importance of countryside, the environment and everyone's right of access to it. They have also identified the terrible state of farming across the country and have highlighted the need to move from the payment of subsidies towards payments for environmental stewardship. At the time of writing an approach called 'Entry Level Agri-Environmental Scheme' (ELAES) is under trial. Lincolnshire is one of the pilot areas and the Conservation Services Team are providing both SMR data and management input into the scheme and will monitor its potential effectiveness. If the scheme is developed across the rest of the UK during the next two to three years, it will have a significant effect as farmers will be paid to demonstrate low-level positive environmental management of their farms.

Whilst it is early days and agri-environment schemes are still very much under development, the pilot scheme proposals suggest that the structure of the scheme will charge farmers with demonstrating that they are undertaking a number of simple environmental measures. An archaeological example might be taking an archaeological site out of arable production and setting it down to grass. For this action an applicant would receive a number of points per set area. On demonstrating that a certain number of points have been attained the applicant would receive the ELAES payment. In parallel to the ELAES a new higher-level scheme is being considered to replace CSS and Environmentally Sensitive Areas.

In addition to the ELAES Lord Haskins has been appointed to carry out a review of the Department of Environment Food and Rural Affairs (DEFRA). At a recent Commons select-committee style briefing from Lord Haskins it was made clear that all mechanisms for the delivery of resources for the rural economy were being reviewed. The environment is to have a higher agenda.

3) <u>Reactive Management - by control</u>: The majority of this work in a Local Authority context sits under the heading of Development Control, where planning legislation and environmental impact regulations are used to mitigate the detrimental effects of development proposals on the historic environment. The controls are reasonably robust but the process is largely reactive and targeted primarily by the desire for development. However, there is some level of proactive management involved as archaeologists have input into the creation of policies for local plans and the county structure plan. The whole plan process is presently changing however with the onset of Community Plans and the level of input for archaeologists into this new planning process is as yet uncertain.

Management By Control – The Development Control Process

Local Government Organisation

We must start by identifying the curatorial system in the study area. The Witham valley from Lincoln to Tattershall passes through five administrative districts. At the west end of the study area is Lincoln City which is advised by its own City Archaeologist. To the south of the river in North Kesteven the archaeological advice is provided through the Community Archaeology programme administered by The Heritage Trust of Lincolnshire. East and West Lindsey to the north of the river receive their curatorial advice from County Archaeologist and development control team of Conservation Services, Lincolnshire County Council. The County Council is also responsible for minerals permissions, overseeing the work of statutory undertakers and national agencies through the environmental impact regulations as well as advising the County Council on its own developments.

District Level Development

Turning first to district matters, these are developments requiring planning permission under the Town and Country Planning legislation and dealt with by District Planning Departments; principally housing and light industrial developments. In North Kesteven, on the southwestern side of the valley (see Fig. 1), such developments are restricted to the edge of the valley in the major villages, examples being Metheringham and Heighington. These settlements developed on the high ground above the Car Dyke. Only Billinghay and Washingborough extended significantly down into the flood plain. Present development land allocations for these settlements are largely used up. We shall have to await the next local plan consultation to assess the threats from these developments in the future.

To the north Cherry Willingham, Fiskerton, Woodhall Spa and Tattershall/Coningsby are all expanding settlements. A few of these, such as Tattershall/Coningsby, as well as Bardney and Southrey, are more low lying, either within the valley itself or on the sands and gravels at the confluence of the Witham and the river Bain. At Fiskerton development has extended down into the valley touching the edge of the Iron Age peat. In the current political and economic climate it is difficult to predict how these settlements will develop, particularly considering recent guidance on levels of residential development and building within flood plains. It is most unlikely that valley deposits will be at risk in the near future from this category of development but, we must not ignore the crests of the valley. Potentially these hold information just as important to understanding the significance of the valley as those remains on the valley floor and as described above, village infill and expansion on both sides of the river will threaten remains in these areas.

There is increased cause for concern over the fate of deposits at the western end of the study area within Lincoln. Here industrial and business development lines the banks of the river and there is very little in the way of archaeological information. There is likely to be significant pressure for the expansion of development in this area if proposals for the Lincoln eastern bypass go ahead.

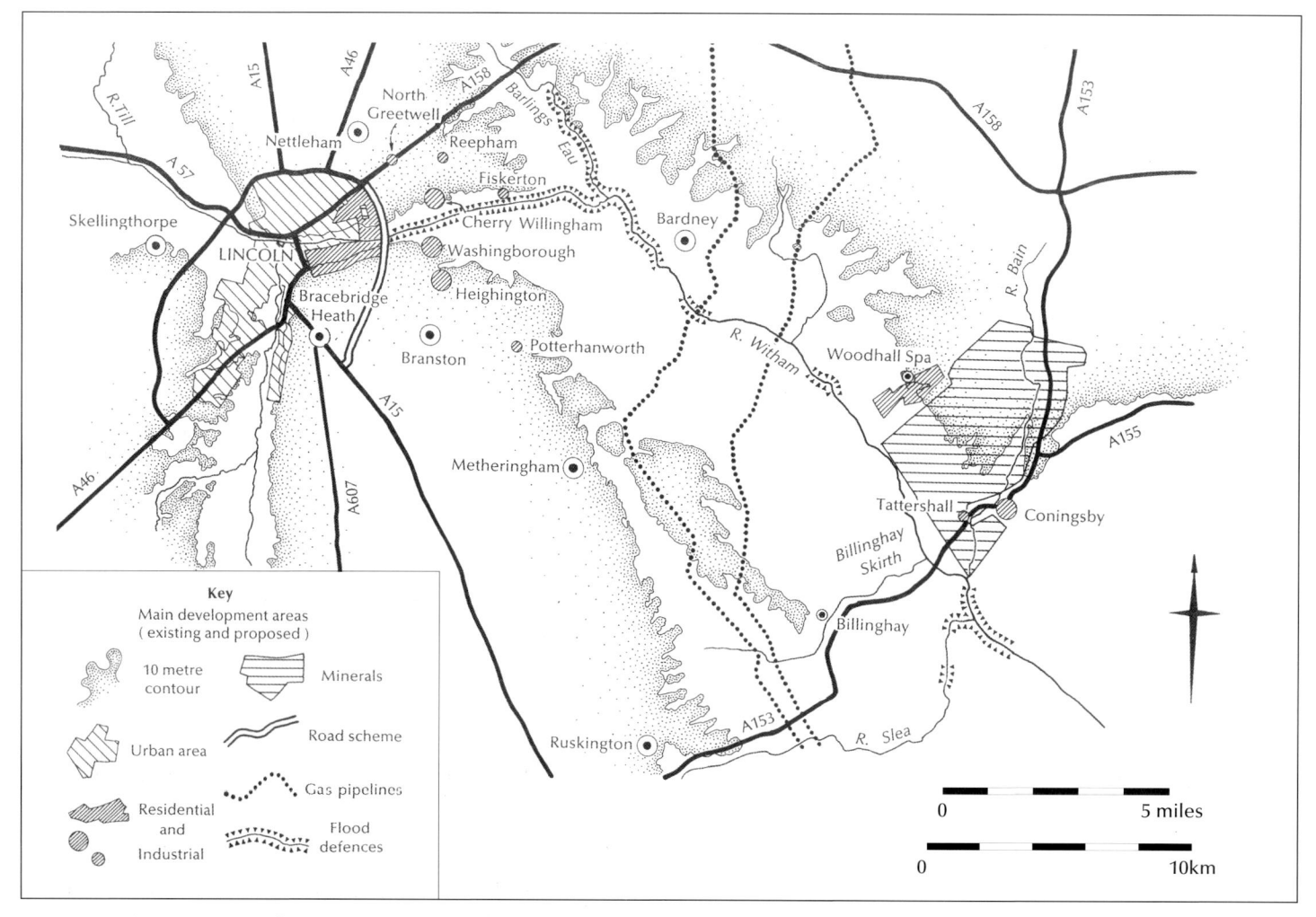

Figure 1 Development issues in the Witham Valley managed through County or District Planning departments include expanding urban and rural settlement, mineral extraction, road schemes, pipelines and flood defences. Drawn by D.W. Hopkins

It should not be forgotten that there are many agricultural developments within the valley such as reservoirs and new farm buildings, which will not be predictable from the local development plans. Some of these require only prior approval applications and have a very short timetable for appraisal but their impact can be considerable (see reservoir to south of river on the aerial photograph on the rear cover). They are also particularly relevant as many of the monastic sites along the valley are in close proximity to farm complexes and apart from the physical impact they can also raise issues of setting which has the potential to affect some of the topics discussed in other papers in this volume.

The matters outlined above are dealt with under the aegis of PPG15 and PPG16, and are adequately regulated through the planning process although the outcomes are still subject to what might best be referred to as 'the fog' of Development Control. This phenomenon includes the vagaries of planning committees, planning officers and planning inspectors whose interpretation of the guidance, and whose priorities, may vary from those of the curatorial archaeologists. This can lead to planning outcomes which prove less than satisfactory for the historic environment or even ignore it altogether. Raising the profile of the study area would be an important step in dispersing this fog.

On the positive side the process delivers a constant stream of information through evaluation, excavation and watching briefs. One recent evaluation in Fiskerton identified a Roman 'hard', a surface for the beaching of boats while loading and unloading, while another at a nearby scrap-yard, enabled the identification and recording of buildings relating to Fiskerton's original manor house sited at the northern end of the causeway, believed to have been associated with Peterborough Abbey. In this latter case, although the developer was initially unenthusiastic about the work, it ultimately benefited him by allowing the archaeological issues to be dealt with prior to development, rather than work being delayed as a result of the site being located in the course of a watching brief. The evaluation of the area also identified more deeply buried prehistoric remains on the site, which were preserved *in situ*.

The planning history of the scrap-yard site was interesting as the applicant appealed against the request for archaeological works, including evaluation, on the site, the justification being that there were no records of archaeology being present on or immediately adjacent to the scrap-yard. The County Archaeologist met with the Planning Inspector on site and described his view of the Witham landscape in antiquity, together with details of the causeway location, the topography and the development of the village. This made the case for the high archaeological potential of the application area, which after consideration was sufficient for the Planning Inspector to dismiss the appeal ... thank goodness the evaluation located archaeology!

County Planning Matters

Mineral extraction operations are also subject to the processes advocated in PPG 16 and to the Environmental Impact Assessment Regulations. In the Witham valley, the principal focus of this industry is the sand and gravel deposits in the area of Tattershall, Kirkby on Bain and Tumby (Fig. 2). The limestone resources on the valley edge at Greetwell should also be considered relevant. Large areas of the landscape have been surveyed as a result of the control of mineral extraction and sites such as the multiple linear ditch system at Greetwell and associated settlement and the Neolithic features at Kirkby on Bain have been excavated and recorded.

Less well defined controls are available for those undertaking work under permitted development rights such as statutory undertakers and national agencies. Although there are various acts that require statutory undertakers to consider archaeology (*e.g.* The Environment Act 1995 - which created the Environment Agency) their responsibilities towards the historic environment are usually limited to vague statements: *e.g.* the Environment Agency must "have regard for the desirability of protecting and conserving buildings, sites and objects of archaeological, architectural, engineering or historic interest". Although some of the vague statements in the acts have been developed and expanded with codes of practice and conservation policies, the strict controls inherent in the planning system are absent and curatorial input is through the Environmental Impact Assessment Regulations and negotiation.

The route between the Hatton and Silk Willoughby gas compressor stations crosses the Witham valley and has resulted in two major gas pipeline projects passing through the valley in the past few years. Transco employs archaeological consultants to carry out desk-based assessments and field evaluations, which may lead to excavations and watching briefs during topsoil stripping and pipe-trench cutting. Despite the requirements within the regulations for full methods of mitigation to be detailed in the Assessment Report the mitigation habitually involves references to further evaluation with no detail about the treatment of specifically identified sites. Most sites are identified at watching brief stage and mitigation is often a last minute issue discussed on site. Publication in relevant journals is rare but the sheer quantity of information from these linear schemes is impressive (seven new sites were located and recorded in 2001). Additionally, pipeline evaluation work has included useful borehole studies of the Witham valley deposits.

Anglian Water has been active in the valley although these works are usually relatively minor involving narrow linear trenches, along the roads or verges. Works usually result in watching briefs and although significant data has been uncovered by Anglian Water across the county, the works have not to date contributed greatly to our knowledge of the Witham valley.

Recently, it has been the works proposed by the Environment Agency which have highlighted the pressures from development upon the archaeology of the valley. The Environment Agency works are programmed to take place over the next five years and involve considerable disturbance along the banks of the river and associated watercourses to north and south. The programme involves raising banks and improving dyke systems as well as the creation of flood storage areas. The extraction of clays and subsequent reservoir creation is taking place and evaluation and recording programmes have been and are being undertaken on the scheme, including detailed discussions regarding avoidance of sites where possible and other mitigation measures where disturbance is unavoidable. A desk based assessment of the project corridor has been carried out as well as specific field evaluation ahead of

Figure 2. Aerial photograph of the confluence of the rivers Bain and Witham near Coningsby. The impact of mineral extraction is clearly demonstrated by the flooded gravel pits and other pressures are evident with RAF airfield and the growing settlements of Tattershall and Coningsby (Top is north).
This image is an extract from The Millennium Map™, ©Getmapping plc

works in sensitive areas. These have included the southern bank of the Witham opposite Fiskerton (to look at the projection of the Fiskerton Causeway) and at Branston Island in advance of the cutting of a new soke dike. A partnership with the Environment Agency has been developed and a satisfactory understanding reached.

Another high impact scheme is currently being developed. Plans for an eastern bypass for Lincoln are nearing completion and a planning application is expected in autumn/winter 2003. The construction of the road would create a corridor of disturbance through the valley from Greetwell, through Washingborough to Canwick and eventually on to the A15. This includes areas of potential bronze-age barrows on the valley floor, Romano-British settlement and multiple linear ditched systems, as well as excellent palaeo-environmental information as indicated by analysis of borehole samples across the valley (see French and Rackham, this volume). At present the plans are to cut through the higher ground and embank the lower sections. The impact on the waterlogged environment will need to be carefully assessed and the advantages (if any) of preserving sites *in situ* considered.

Conclusion

So what can we conclude? First is that the threats to the valley from development are many but localised. The major impacts will be from linear schemes such as roads and pipelines and in particular the works of the Environment Agency on the river itself. To a lesser extent mineral extraction and other forms of excavation, whether that be for materials or irrigation, could impact on some of the better sites and areas within the valley. Housing and industry are a threat within settlement cores, particularly at Lincoln where there is likely to be further industrial development pressure once the new bypass is constructed.

The strength of the present system is the robust control offered by planning legislation. It has taken a decade and a half to develop the present archaeological cultural resource management process and in particular the associated development control system. This is now reasonably well resourced and working very well with most of the processes and policies enshrined in local and structure plans. Other areas of legislation ensure curatorial input into the vast majority of development schemes. Generally, good relationships exist between the curators, planners, contractors and agencies within the county and the existence of the county council also offers the overview to curate effectively a study area of this size and administrative complexity, although we may now ask how long this situation will last in the light of regionalisation and changes to the planning system. Although not yet complete (it is a very large county!) a comprehensive and well developed sites and monuments record is a strength, as are the very experienced and professional archaeological contracting units working in the county. Also, a number of fora were set up in the early 1990s where archaeological problems are aired, solutions discussed and local standards agreed. These are all recorded within the *Lincolnshire Archaeological Handbook* which helps to enable a consistent approach to be achieved.

Another Lincolnshire strength lies in the multidisciplinary nature of the Conservation Services Team of the County Council. Having ecologists, tree experts, buildings professionals and countryside managers in the same team as the archaeologists, is leading to a number of more 'joined-up' holistic approaches to projects as demonstrated in the recent Wolds Interpretation Strategy. This is an approach which will in due course be applied to the Witham valley. In addition to the holistic approach of the team members the network of colleagues gives access to many additional specialists (*e.g.* the Farming and Wildlife Group advisors) who want archaeological input into their schemes and vice versa. Two such examples are recent Countryside Stewardship Schemes at Greetwell and Fiskerton.

The multi-disciplinary approach also identifies funding streams that might not initially have been sought by archaeologists. In the last two or three years, projects funded under Objective 5b and in particular Leader II have included archaeological priorities. A further strength is that the government is focusing on the damage caused by farming to environmental/cultural assets *e.g.* archaeology and new schemes will pay farmers for environmental stewardship.

The weaknesses of the development control process lie in its reactivity and the lack of enforcement in the controls of permitted development. Schemes can be highly political and subject to their own momentum; the 'fog' of development control can descend on the best planned schemes. Work is sporadic, academically untargeted and lacking in overall synthesis. In addition cultural resource management resources are limited and vulnerable to reorganisations and cuts.

We must not ignore the opportunities inherent within the Development Control process. The evaluation of proposed development sites has and will continue to provide new and important information. The same is true, not only for work carried out for statutory undertakers but also by statutory undertakers. Borehole information can be particularly relevant and contribute to the study of the valley and while we cannot necessarily justify analysis of environmental information through the planning process, we can work with agencies to collect the data for further study. All this information should feed into a research programme for the valley so that future development can feed off the results of that research.

For The Future

The threats will not disappear but the weaknesses can be recognised and minimised while the opportunities are maximised. There are several elements to embrace:

- Data Collection – A huge amount of Witham valley data requires collection. Some surveys are already taking place in the Fiskerton area, collecting data by fieldwalking, aerial photography (including multi-spectral, topographic survey with LIDAR) borehole and auger survey *etc*. These data-sets must be collected, interpreted and drawn together. Similar surveys are needed for other parts of the valley
- Enhancing the Sites and Monuments Record – the data once collected should be made available to all through the county SMR. The SMR has the ability to take many types of data-set and manipulate them through MAPINFO GIS. This information should then be used to inform several other areas of work.
- Intrusive Archaeological work – excavation is required at various key points in the study area in order to understand the depositional sequences, levels of preservation and settlement patterns.
- Synthesising all existing data – there is an urgent need to synthesise the information already captured through small scale development control projects. Desk top studies recently carried out for the Environment Agency by Pre-Construct Archaeology have begun the task but there will be much additional data held by all those involved in the project. This data needs to be assessed, ordered and synthesised (*e.g.* Dr Bob Bewley of English Heritage is reviewing and plotting all the existing aerial photography of the valley). Resources are also needed to process data previously considered to be beyond the remit of development control work.
- Monitoring – the condition of the valley and its archaeology should be routinely monitored. Recent work has raised the possibility that we may have lost in the region of 0.5 metres of archaeology from the causeway in only 20 years (*pers comm*. Rackham). This loss is caused by desiccation of the peat deposits due to drainage and ploughing breaking up the soil and vegetation cover. The archaeology then simply blows away. If we do not change something soon, the "answer my friend" will literally "be blowing in the wind"! We must start to monitor as soon as possible, including monitoring the effects of our own management processes on the archaeology of the valley.
- Research Agenda – one of the most pressing needs is for a detailed research agenda covering the wide range of archaeological issues within the valley, which can then be used to inform development control decisions and future research proposals. A well designed research framework will provide the necessary academic justification to underpin the advice given by curators and will target developer funded work more effectively.
- Landscape Character Assessment – a historic landscape character assessment should be carried out for Lincolnshire and would put the valley in a clear context. This work should be incorporated with a natural areas landscape character assessment.
- Site Designation – most importantly, the profile of the archaeological potential of the landscape must be raised so that its relevance to the whole community is evident to planners, elected members and all those working in development control. Some form of identifying designation should be created for the study area. Lincolnshire has a Rural Action Zone which achieves a similar role for a wide range of interests in South Holland. Perhaps we could create an Archaeological Action Zone, an Area of Outstanding Archaeological Importance, or even an Archaeological Park? None of these terms are particularly original outside archaeology, but all are worthy of consideration. It may help to be more inclusive … perhaps designating an Area of Significant Environmental Assets, an Environmental Action Zone, or just sticking to the tried and tested 'Historic Environment' Action Zone.
- Management Strategies - once the area is designated in an appropriate way, the academic research agenda can be adapted into management strategies to be adopted as supplementary planning guidance, enshrined in local plans, local development frameworks or spatial strategies. These will provide a planning framework for advice from curators to local authorities and will also increase the weight carried by this historic landscape at appeals or inquiries. The strategies would then be used to guide cultural resource management and the limited financial resources we have available to best effect.

Bibliography

Cabinet Office, 2002, Farming and Food: A Sustainable Future (Report of The Policy Commission, Chairman, Sir Donald Curry CBE) (London, HMSO).

Countryside and Rights of Way Act, 2000 (London, HMSO).

Department of the Enviroment and Department of National Heritage, 1994, Planning and Policy Guidance Note 15: Planning And The Historic Environment (London, HMSO).

Department of the Environment, 1990, Planning and Policy Guidance Note 16: Archaeology and Planning (London, HMSO).

Department of the Environment, Transport and the Regions (DETR), 2000, Planning and Policy Guidance Note 3: Housing (London, HMSO).

Department of the Environment, Transport and the Regions (DETR), 2000, Our Countryside: The Future - A Fair Deal for England (The 'Rural White Paper') (London, HMSO).

Department of Transport, Local Government and the Regions (DTLR), 2001, Planning and Policy Guidance Note 25: Development And Flood Risk (London, HMSO).

Environment Act, 1995, chap 25 (London, HMSO).

Lincolnshire County Council, 1997, *The Lincolnshire Archaeological Handbook* (Lincoln, Lincolnshire County Council).

Lincolnshire County Council, 2001, *The Lincolnshire Wolds - Interpretation Strategy* (Lincoln, Lincolnshire County Council).

Palmer-Brown, M., 2000, Medieval Manor, Nelson Road, Fiskerton, Lincolnshire (unpublished archaeological excavation report, Pre-Construct Archaeology).

Palmer-Brown, M., 1994, Perrins Cottages, Fiskerton, Lincolnshire (unpublished archaeological field evaluation report, Pre-Construct Archaeology).

Palmer-Brown, M., 1999, Land off Nelson Road, Fiskerton, Lincolnshire (unpublished archaeological field evaluation report, Pre-Construct Archaeology).

Rylatt, J., 2001, Lower Witham Flood Defence Improvement Scheme, Part1 – 19 Sections of Flood Defences (Phase 2 and 3 Works 2001/2-2002/3) River Witham and Barlings Eau, Lincolnshire (unpublished archaeological desk-based assessment report, Pre-Construct Archaeology).

Rylatt, J., 2002a, Lower Witham Flood Defence Improvement Scheme, Part 2 – 32 Sections of Flood Defences (Phase 2 and 3 Works, 2003/4-2005/6) River Witham, Barlings Eau, Billinghay Skirth, Kyme Eau, Lincolnshire (unpublished archaeological desk-based assessment report, Pre-Construct Archaeology).

Rylatt, J., 2002b, Lower Witham Flood Defence Improvement Scheme (Phase 4 Works), Part 3 – Branston Delph, Nocton Delph, Metheringham Delph and Timberland Delph and 3 Sections of the Car Dyke, Lincolnshire (unpublished archaeological desk-based assessment report, Pre-Construct Archaeology).

Rylatt, J., 2002c, Report on a Programme of Archaeological Fieldwork Undertaken on Branston Island, Branston, Lincolnshire (unpublished report, Pre-Construct Archaeology).

Town and Country Planning (Environmental Impact Assessment) Regulations 1999, SI 1999 No 293 (London, HMSO).

Town and Country Planning (General Permitted Development) Order 1995 S.I.1995 No.418 (London, HMSO).

Town and Country Planning Act, 1990 (London, HMSO).

MANAGEMENT THROUGH OTHER MECHANISMS

by Dave Went

Introduction

For many of us in the archaeological profession it does not seem very long ago that we felt like the poor relations of the other environmental disciplines represented in the planning system. Nowadays, under the Town and Country Planning (TCP) legislation and the accompanying policies and guidance, it is routine for developments affecting the archaeological resource to be preceded by assessments, evaluations or major excavations, or for development plans to be modified to mitigate or avoid damage. These procedures may, as at Fiskerton, provide significant new information in line with research aspirations (Bonnor and Catney, this volume). But do these mechanisms alone provide enough support for the protection and management of the archaeological resource, particularly in such an important landscape as the central Witham valley?

Planning Policy Guidance 16 (PPG16 Archaeology and Planning) emphasises the desirability of preserving important archaeological sites, and many large scale developments will also now be subject to the TCP Regulations (1999), which require advanced consideration of archaeology as part of wider Environmental Impact Assessments. Archaeology has become a major concern for the Environment Agency (Environment Act 1995) and has been incorporated into the legislation governing many other statutory undertakers – for example the Water Industry Act 1991 and the Electricity Act 1989.

Despite the best efforts of many development control (DC) professionals working to implement these regulations and guidelines, there are still serious shortcomings in the system. For one thing, in all these mechanisms, archaeology is but one consideration competing for attention. Other concerns – economic considerations, social factors or technological limitations – are given similar or greater weight and may prevail against the advice of professional archaeologists who, after all, are rarely the final arbiters in the decision-making process. For another, these mechanisms are largely threat related and deal with immediate concerns rather than long term management. The hard pressed DC archaeologist is faced with the more urgent task of preventing or mitigating the effects of development, and only rarely has the luxury of being able to set in place long term conservation initiatives for the archaeological remains.

Furthermore, there are the significant threats to the archaeological resource which fall beyond the normal scope of development control measures. These are many and various - including permitted development under General Development Order use-classes (such as agricultural or forestry buildings and some forms of industrial building, utility provision and mineral extraction), and less obvious threats such as unregulated archaeological investigations or ill-considered conservation work. By far the greatest threat, however, is agricultural use and change. A few stark findings from English Heritage's *Monuments at Risk Survey* (MARS) serve to illustrate the point. Agriculture has been the single greatest cause of unrecorded loss of archaeological sites – responsible for 10% of all cases of monument destruction between 1945-95 and for some 30% of piecemeal, cumulative damage in the same period (Darvill and Fulton 1998). Most of this damage results from ongoing cultivation, which is difficult to control (see below), but much can be also attributed to new ploughing of former pasture, farm amalgamation and intensification and the creation of new agricultural reservoirs and buildings.

More relevant to the central Witham valley are the findings of the English Heritage's 'Monuments at Risk in England's Wetlands (MAREW) Project', commissioned from Exeter University in 2000. Drawing on the results of the four wetland surveys (undertaken in the Somerset Levels, the Fens, the raised wetlands of North East England, and the Humberside Levels between 1973 and 2001) and other data, this desktop assessment identified the average density of archaeological sites in all England's wetlands, the rate of loss and the reasons underlying this destruction. The results (Coles and Olivier 2001, Olivier 2002) make for uncomfortable reading. Without providing much direct information on the situation in the central Witham valley (after all, the survey of the East Anglian Fens was curtailed not far inland from Boston) they do indicate disturbing trends and parallels. At least 50% of the original extent of lowland peatland has been lost in the last 50 years. Estimating an average density of sites in England's wetlands of one in every 100 hectares indicates an original population of at least 13,400 monuments, well over half of which will have been destroyed or damaged without any archaeological knowledge gained.

Surprisingly perhaps, peat cutting, the most visible mode of destruction, is no longer the main threat. Far more serious for the important waterlogged and structural remains is the impact of drainage – the cutting of drains, the drying of land for agriculture and the consequential wastage of desiccated peat from cultivated land.

All these threats are of great concern for the well-being of the internationally important archaeology present in the Witham valley. Development control cannot provide a solution in every case, and we must therefore look to the other mechanisms available, assess their effectiveness, and if needs be, seek to enhance their suitability for the task in hand.

Statutory Designation

The underlying philosophy of scheduling (the process of protecting nationally important archaeological sites under, most recently, the Ancient Monuments and Archaeological Areas Act 1979) is that these cultural assets are not to be 'traded' against development needs, or damaged by any works unauthorised by the Secretary of State. The emphasis is, therefore, very different to that found in the 'cut and thrust' of planning debates, and provides a clarity and direction based solely on the presumption that the protection of the archaeological site sits at the very top of the agenda. This is not to say that scheduled monuments may not be exploited for their evidential potential, rather that releasing this 'cultural capital' must be judged within a longer time-span and against a more systematic and considered research framework than those afforded by the planning process. Neither can scheduling be said to provide a complete solution to the issues of site preservation – far from it. English Heritage (as the Secretary of State's adviser in these matters) will rarely be able to insist that certain damaging activities cease - most notably ongoing ploughing to normal depth. However, the act of scheduling provides a clear statement of a site's national importance, which enables English Heritage to control damage and, together with a growing number of partners in governmental and non-governmental agencies, to direct resources towards improved management.

Since the late 1980s English Heritage's Monuments Protection Programme has acted as the Secretary of State's principal adviser on scheduling. The MPP provides recommendations to the Department for Culture Media and Sport based on a series of national assessment and evaluation programmes, followed by further research and field work undertaken by a small group of archaeologists working across the counties of England. Some of these evaluation projects (particularly the more recent industrial and military themes) have been tackled through new research at the national level. But most monuments classes, the more traditional assortment of archaeological sites, were evaluated from information held in county Sites and Monuments Records, and assessed against the Secretary of State's non-statutory criteria (survival, potential, group value, archaeological and historical documentation and amenity value).

For the greater part, the work of MPP in the Witham Valley has been guided by the exhaustive work carried out by Julia Wise, then Lincolnshire County Council SMR Assistant. Using information from the SMR, supplemented by additional primary research on all monument classes, a ranked scoring was achieved. A list of sites to be considered for scheduling was then created through discussions between David Stocker, EH Inspector, and Steve Catney, County Archaeologist. Over the last ten years we have been following up these desk-based and professional recommendations. Most of this work has been undertaken by a single MPP Archaeologist, Alison Peach, within her greater responsibility for scheduling research across the rest of Lincolnshire, Cambridgeshire and (latterly) Essex.

The pattern of MPP work is shown by taking a somewhat unscientific slice along the Witham valley - extending up to 10km into the broken landscape at the foot of the Wolds to the east and a similar if slightly broader area towards the limestone border to the west and around the fen basin to the south (Fig. 1). Within this area the combination of national and county-based assessments revealed 118 sites of known or potential national importance, including 48 which were already scheduled and required revision.

At the time of writing there are now 78 scheduled monuments in the area. 24 of these are still unreviewed old schedulings, but 54 are modern MPP schedulings, and two thirds of these have been scheduled for the first time by the MPP. Ten further sites have been visited and researched through MPP, but for various reasons (recorded in MPP 'Alternative Action' reports), have not been recommended for scheduling.

So MPP has researched, visited and made recommendations for 64 of the 118 sites

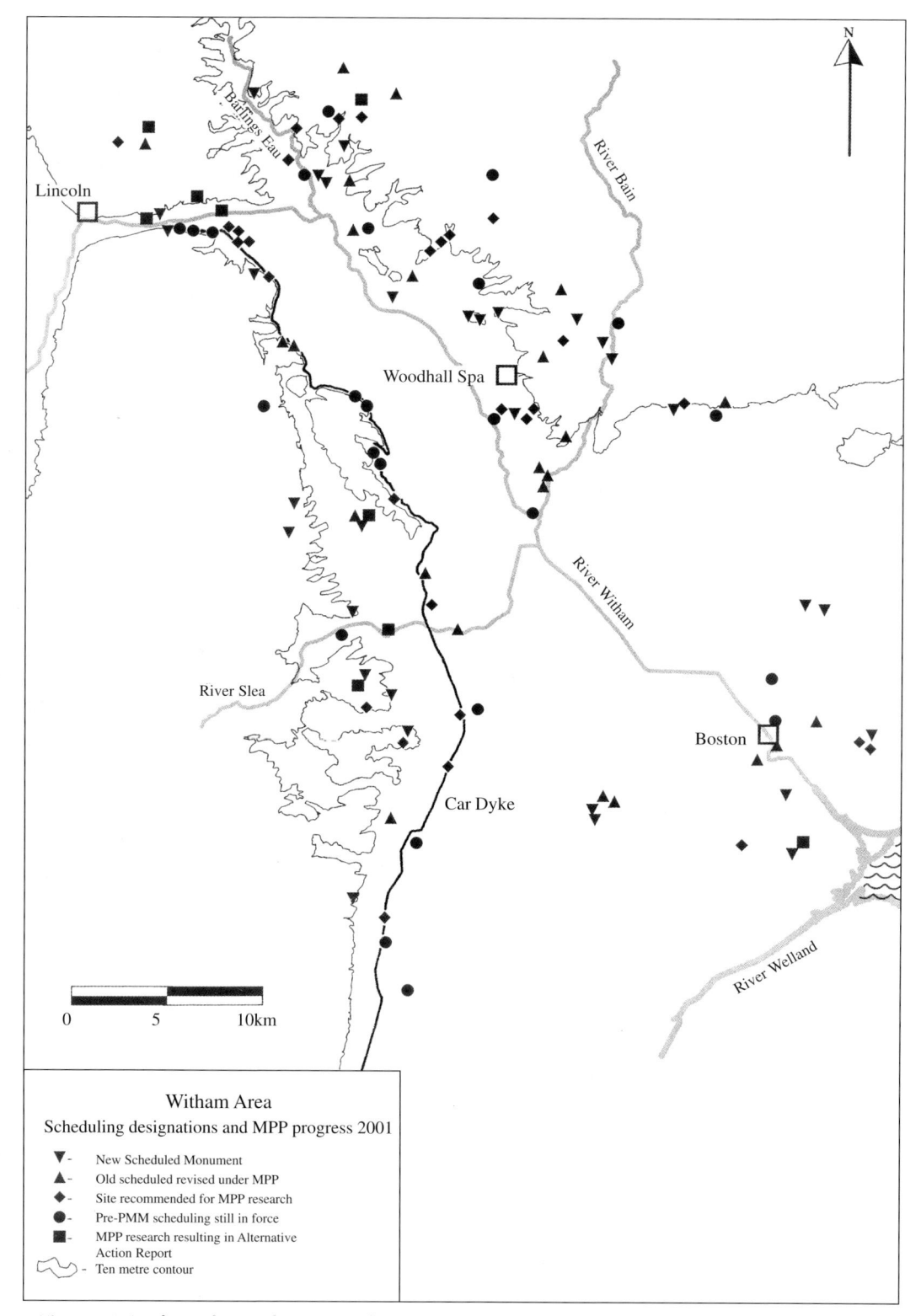

Figure 1 Archaeological sites and monuments in and around the Witham valley that are scheduled or considered for scheduling.
Map compiled by M. Bennet, based on the Lincolnshire Sites and Monuments Record.

representing the nationally important resource as it was presented through the desk-based evaluation process, and the state of play is that two thirds of this resource is currently protected by scheduling - mostly either new or updated designations, with a number of early schedulings still providing protection but awaiting revision.

Scheduling designations now cover most of the monastic institutions relating to the known or

Figure 2 Aerial view of part of the Barlings/Stainfield barrow cemetery, recently evaluated and scheduled as an ancient monument. North to the right. NMR SF3213/6 26-JUL-86. © Chris Cox

postulated causeways across the Witham (Everson and Stocker, this volume). Kirkstead Abbey, Haverholme Priory and Barlings Abbey are protected by existing designations, the latter pending a comprehensive review in the light of recent work by Everson and Stocker. The old schedulings of the abbeys at Bardney and Tupholme, the priory sites at Walcott (Catley) and South Kyme and the nunnery at Stainfield have already seen substantial revision under the MPP. Stixwould Priory is newly scheduled, as are the Bishop's Palace at Nettleham, smaller institutions such as Seney Place monastic retreat (Southrey) and the grange at Roughton, and a sizable number of other secular and ecclesiastical monuments and sites to either side of the Witham.

Earlier monuments, dating from the Romano-British and prehistoric periods, are not so well represented in the schedule. A number of early sites are already scheduled along the margins and hinterland of the valley, mainly Roman and principally related to the line of the Car Dyke. A few of these have been revised by MPP, such as the Roman barrows at Revesby and the Tattershall Thorpe defended enclosure. Some, including the Walcott long barrow and the known part of the Barlings/Stainfield barrow cemetery (Fig. 2) are new to the schedule. The list of Romano-British and prehistoric sites in the areas is not extensive, however, but the pattern of sites both evaluated and scheduled reveals the reason for this uneven coverage.

Most of the recorded RB and prehistoric sites lie above the 5m contour, which marks the edge of the valley floor fens. Looking at the evaluated sites by period (Fig. 3) the pattern is clearly dominated by medieval and post-medieval settlement on the fringes of the valley floor - a line of moated sites, village and churchyard crosses and monastic sites marching along the limestone above the level of the early Iron Age inundation to the south west, and to the east a similar mixture set along the more broken slopes falling from the Wolds, including, of course, the Lindsey monasteries seated on the fen edge. The MPP, and its predecessors in English Heritage and the Department of Environment, have been drawn towards highly visible earthworks and structures, in line with the developing country archaeological record, and demonstrate the same inevitable bias towards the medieval and (with sites such as the bridges across waterways in and around Boston, the Sibsey windmill and Dogdyke pumping station) later periods. Obviously, buried archaeological deposits are taken into account in

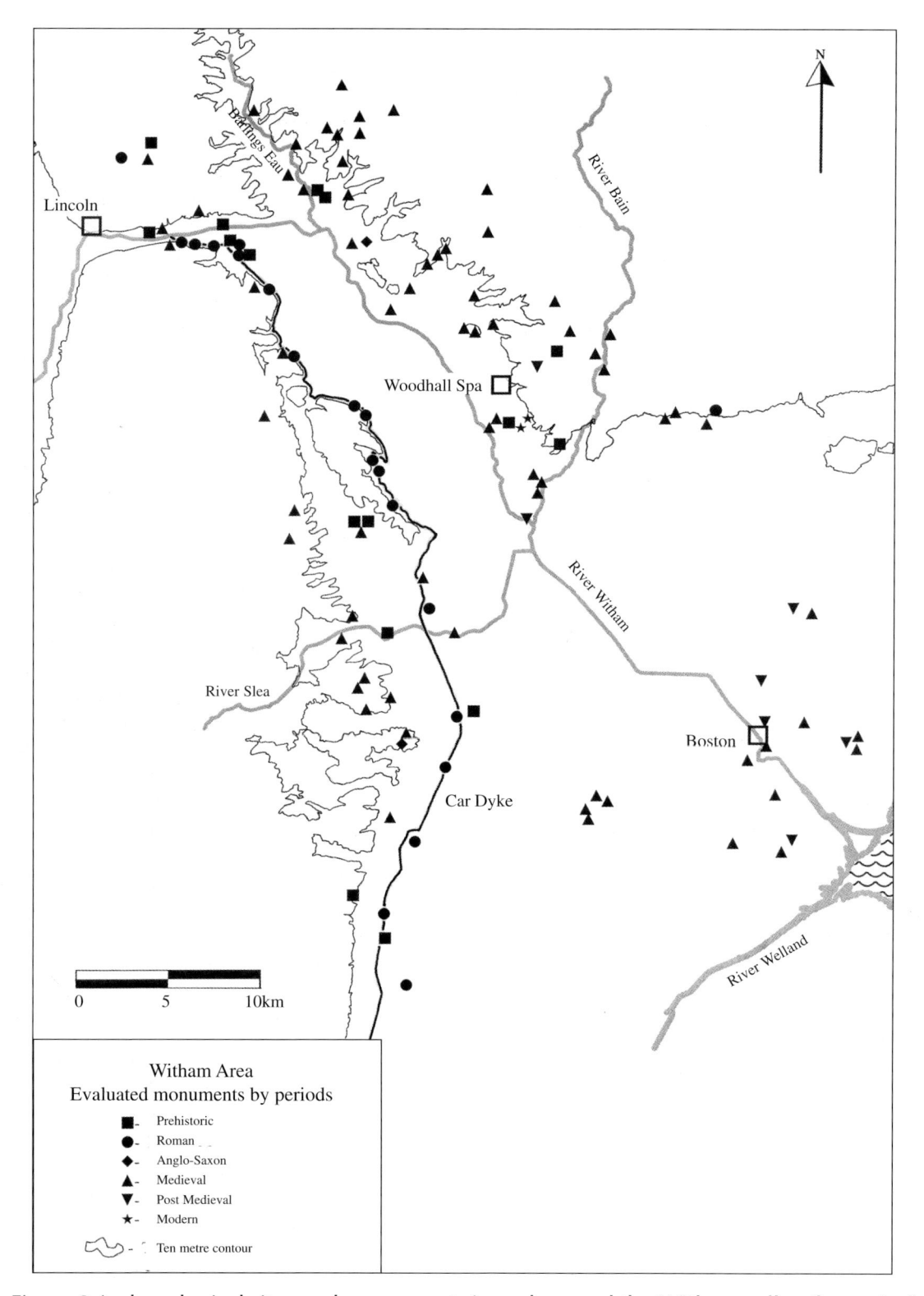

Figure 3 Archaeological sites and monuments in and around the Witham valley (by period) evaluated by the Monuments Protection Programme.
Map compiled by M. Bennet, based on the Lincolnshire Sites and Monuments Record

these schedulings, and on some sites (particularly the few earlier sites represented on the schedule) this evidence provides the substantial part of the information required to justify designation. But all these sites have one thing in common - a high level of definition, whether as earthworks, cropmarks or excavated evidence, and this enables these sites to be identified, characterised, scored against the national criteria and, ultimately, managed as scheduled monuments.

The archaeological potential within the valley floor is enormous, as the contributors to this volume have clearly demonstrated but there are sometimes significant difficulties in protecting this potential through scheduling. In order for the Secretary of State to add a site to the schedule it must be demonstrated that it is of national importance. It could be argued, perhaps quite easily, that the totality of the buried prehistoric landscape along the Witham is of national importance but, unfortunately, there are other constraints on the designation of scheduled monuments. Scheduled monuments have to be 'works' – a broad definition which can encompass anything from the Bronze Age saltern at Billingborough to the WWII airfield defences at Woodhall Spa. However, despite protracted arguments from the MPP, the legal definition still does not include scatters of pottery, lithics or metal work without the known presence or reasonable assumption of associated made-made features. Monuments have to be defined in other ways to achieve designation – specifically in terms of their morphological characteristics (in order to identify the type of site and evaluate its importance against the total population of comparable sites in England), details of extent (in order to map the monument as an entity) and evidence of good archaeological survival – all aspects which are difficult to define due to the masking effects of fenland peat and alluvium. Where this definition is lacking, the best that MPP can do is to provide 'Alternative Action' reports, stipulating the reasons why scheduling cannot be proposed and advocating further investigation. Six of the ten AA reports for the Witham valley reports concern prehistoric sites - all barrow cemeteries situated on the lower slopes of the valley, including some (Fiskerton, Anwick, Walcott) related to the ritual deposits, monastic institutions and the known or postulated causeways. Assuming that field work progresses in this area and new information is forthcoming, we would be delighted to reassess the scheduling position.

Management

Once identified and designated, scheduled monuments require management, as do any archaeological sites. In some cases management may be quite minimal - little more than routine monitoring and limited occasional grant assistance for minor conservation work. In others, the conservation needs may be more pronounced, in which case the scheduling helps to target management funding, both from EH and elsewhere, and dictate a more active approach to curation. The examples of the Witham Abbeys now under direct management by the Heritage Trust of Lincolnshire (David Start, this volume) exemplify this approach.

Conversely, scheduling can follow in the wake of management initiatives, supporting decisions about national importance and sustainability arising from new archaeological research. The recent work on the Car Dyke is a prime example. With English Heritage funding, Archaeological Project Services (Heritage Trust of Lincolnshire) have recently completed a synthesis of the archaeological record along the line of the dyke, and undertaken a full condition survey with management recommendations (Simmons & Cope-Faulkner, forthcoming). MPP is set to follow up this work in 2002-3; not only revising and extending the existing scheduled sections (of which there are nine in the area of the central Witham valley), but also adding new sections which reflect its course along the southern margin of the Witham fens and, crucially, including adjacent or overlapping cropmark sites where the relationship to the dyke provides points of particular interest. This process demonstrates how a well-considered project can lead directly towards the increased legal protection of archaeological sites, and will certainly provide some insights into the possible management outcomes of any future, broader archaeological projects in the Witham valley.

Scheduling alone cannot provide an answer to all the threats which impinge on nationally important sites, although it can be the catalyst for significant conservation gain. Scheduling focusses attention on the monument in all manner of decision-making affecting the landscape. English Heritage can, and does, influence the wider settings of monuments, especially when proposed developments in the area would have a direct effect on the preservation or appreciation of the remains. This can be of particular importance in wetland environs where dewatering, or deliberate flooding, are notable threats. Other agencies, whose primary interests are not archaeological, are left in no doubt of the significance of these sites, should they propose works which would have a damaging effect.

Agri-Environment Schemes

More importantly, the designation provides the impetus to engage with other organisations and agencies in the search for collaborative conservation ventures. In the rural landscape of the Witham valley, where agricultural practices and drainage works are such a particular threat to archaeological survival, such collaboration is vital.

Government agri-environment schemes have operated in England since 1987 and, with the development of Integrated Management Plans under the Agricultural Development Service (ADAS) in the 1990s, these schemes have embodied an increasingly holistic approach to environmental and cultural landscape. The two principal tools for landscape management, Environmentally Sensitive Areas (ESA) and the Countryside Stewardship Scheme (CSS) are now administered by the English Rural Development Programme (ERDP), part of the Department of Environment, Food and Rural Affairs, and provide a range of grants and incentives to farmers who are prepared to maintain and enhance the rural environment.

Increasingly, these resources are being used to assist with the sort of archaeological problems highlighted by MARS, the *Monuments at Risk Survey*, and MAREW, its more recent extension to include wetland concerns. The benefits accrue, in part, as the by-products of schemes, such as arable reversion or stock level control, which are intended mainly to promote biological diversity; also from the 'cross-compliance' conditions imposed on any recipient of Agri-environment funding – whereby a breach in one area of environmental legislation (including the Ancient Monuments and Archaeological Areas Act 1979) may result in the withdrawal of support for other initiatives. However, the ERDP has also developed policies which place the historic environment on an equal footing with other environmental concerns (Middleton 2002) and allow schemes to be formulated which specifically address the needs of archaeological conservation.

In the coming decade the importance of such schemes in determining the survival of archaeological sites and landscapes, such as those in the Witham valley, cannot be overestimated. The Common Agricultural Policy (CAP), formulated in the post-war period to protect the industry and provide cheaper food, is now under attack from many quarters as its true cost, in terms of environmental damage and the tax burden of farm subsidy, is assessed. Furthermore a UK farming crisis, exacerbated by the flood of cheap arable produce from the former Eastern Bloc and the disastrous effects of the recent foot and mouth epidemic, is in full swing, with farm incomes at their lowest point for a generation. Changes are required and the UK Government is at the forefront of the campaign for change within European farming practice. The Rural Development Regulation (Agenda 2000) provided for the redirection of a significant slice of production subsidy for intensive farming (£1.6 billion over six years) towards the objective of a well-managed, diverse and environmentally sound landscape, capable of underpinning the rural economy, attracting tourism and inward investment and enhancing the quality of life for those who visit or inhabit the countryside. A substantial portion of this money is already available for Agri-environment schemes, and English Heritage will not be alone in campaigning for more reforms at the Government's mid-term review in 2003 - promoting still greater consideration for schemes which sustain and enhance the historic landscape and benefit the rural economy.

The potential for the improved management of archaeological sites in the Witham valley is considerable - where such agri-environment schemes provide realistic incentives to farmers searching for cost-effective alternatives to intensive production. The internationally important archaeological landscape of the central Witham must surely rank amongst the most worthy recipients of these schemes. The difficulty we face is in defining the most significant areas of the archaeological resource (below the peat) in order to target these resources effectively. Scheduling helps, but is equally dependent on detailed archaeological knowledge, which is yet to be acquired for most of the formerly inundated valley. Knowledge is the crucial precursor to management and it is to be hoped that the recent attention on the Witham valley is just the starting point for a wide range of necessary research.

Proposals For Future Work:

The basic outline for archaeological research is provided by Everson and others in this volume.

The MPP's contribution will be to press forward with the remaining body of sites evaluated for scheduling in the Witham landscape and to assess any new information which comes to light through any forthcoming research. Areas defined as being of national importance, or having the potential to be so designated, can then be promoted within existing and developing agri-environment schemes and other conservation initiatives. A future extension of English Heritage's Historic Landscape Characterisation (HLC) programme to Lincolnshire will provide a new and useful framework for pursuing this objective.

A broader conservation strategy should be investigated during the progress of the Witham Archaeological project, not only identifying the archaeological landscape but also investigating the current economic structure of the agricultural industry in the area. Fenland farming has some peculiarities which work against the adoption of agri-environment schemes. For example, arable reversion may not be an attractive alternative to comparatively high value root crops, the deep cultivation for which is a particular threat to soil stability and archaeological survival. A clearer understanding of the pattern of agriculture alongside the Witham is a vital precondition of any strategic planning for the management of the archaeological resource.

Bibliography

Coles, B. and Olivier, A., 2001, *The heritage management of Wetlands in Europe*, EAC occasional paper 1/ WARP occasional paper 16.

Darvill, T. and Fulton, A.,1998, *MARs: The Monuments at Risk Survey of England, 1995* (Bournemouth University & English Heritage).

Middleton, R., 2002, 'Historic Environment, Agri-Environment Schemes', *Conservation Bulletin* 42, 16-21 (English Heritage).

Olivier, A., 2002, 'England's Wetlands: monuments at risk', *Conservation Bulletin* 42, 40-45 (English Heritage).

Simmons, B.B. and Cope-Faulkner, P., forthcoming, *The Car Dyke: Past Work, Current State, Future Possibilities*, Lincolnshire Archaeology and Heritage Reports Series (Heritage Trust of Lincolnshire).

CONSERVATION OF EXCAVATED FINDS

by Rob White

This seminar provided an opportunity to reflect on the level of care which has been afforded archaeological material recovered from the river Witham and its environs in recent decades, and to propose a strategy for dealing with any future items or assemblages.

A proposed framework for a schedule of care for such material should:

- be viable, seeking only *in the first instance* to balance the material's long-term integrity with relatively risk free access to it, and;

- be equitable with respect to the various project partners involved in the scheme, where clear and transparent delineation of responsibility between those who generate the archive and those who receive it, in accordance with published standards, will inform the description of accurate specifications.

Conservation work which has already been undertaken on elements of material recovered from the Witham and its banks, can best be described as variable. The Bronze Age log-boat discovered at Short Ferry near Fiskerton in 1958 is one such item which helps to demonstrate this. The exceptional preservation of the boat in the waterlogged and likely anoxic burial environment is in stark contrast to its condition many years later on display in Lincoln's City and County Museum (and now in storage during redevelopment of those displays). Classic and spectacular deterioration of the waterlogged oak, with extensive and irrecoverable longitudinal splitting and warping of (in particular) the outer layers is evident (see Cadbury this volume, Fig. 1). This observation is not intended to lay blame anywhere; awareness of the need for, and facilities for the delivery of such work, were not in evidence to the extent they now are. What it does provide is a sharp reminder of the potential effect of uncontrolled post-excavation drying on such material.

In contrast to this lack of appropriate care, the somewhat over zealous treatment afforded a significant proportion of the metalwork which has arrived in the museum collection through various routes, has also had a detrimental effect. Too great a level of intervention, often administered by well meaning and enthusiastic but misguided amateurs, has had the objective of stripping away deposition accretion in a rather indiscriminate manner. This has resulted in potentially information rich layers of surface deterioration (containing, for example, evidence for decorative surface coatings) being lost, leaving the rather stripped and shiny metalwork beneath.

Some materials have, of course, received a high level of appropriate conservation investment. Spectacular finds such as the Witham Shield, now on display in the British Museum, have benefited from the expertise and resources which such organisations are able to draw upon.

Guidance on the approach to conservation of material which may be recovered as part of this scheme in the future might be derived by examining the way in which the most recent large assemblage from the Witham (prior to Pre-Construct Archaeology's recent phase of works in 2001) was treated. Naomi Field's 1981 excavation at Fiskerton produced a remarkable group of artefacts (the significance of which has been reported elsewhere in this publication) which yielded a diverse and engaging set of conservation and forensic opportunities. The ferrous structures in particular convey something of the potential ritual nature of their deposition. The swords, for example, have wonderfully evocative mineralised evidence for their deposition sheathed, and within scabbards (Figure 1).

Some of the ferrous material from this group displays an extremely advanced level of deterioration, with pseudomorphic evidence for original features surviving through extensive mineralisation (Figure 2). However, the accuracy with which this process has been able to preserve elements of original morphology, is nothing short of stunning. Contrasting with this very advanced level of deterioration are ferrous objects which have very robust structures. They are virtually unaltered and have only superficial surface degradation, suggesting potentially complex localised burial environments, and further underpinning the essential nature of the work currently being undertaken by Ian Panter of English Heritage (Panter 2002). This has been concerned with raising the profile of the potential for archaeological science projects which could arise from and/or be informed by the type of observations a conservator is able to make, but be delivered in partnership with other appropriate

Conservation Of Excavated Finds by Rob White

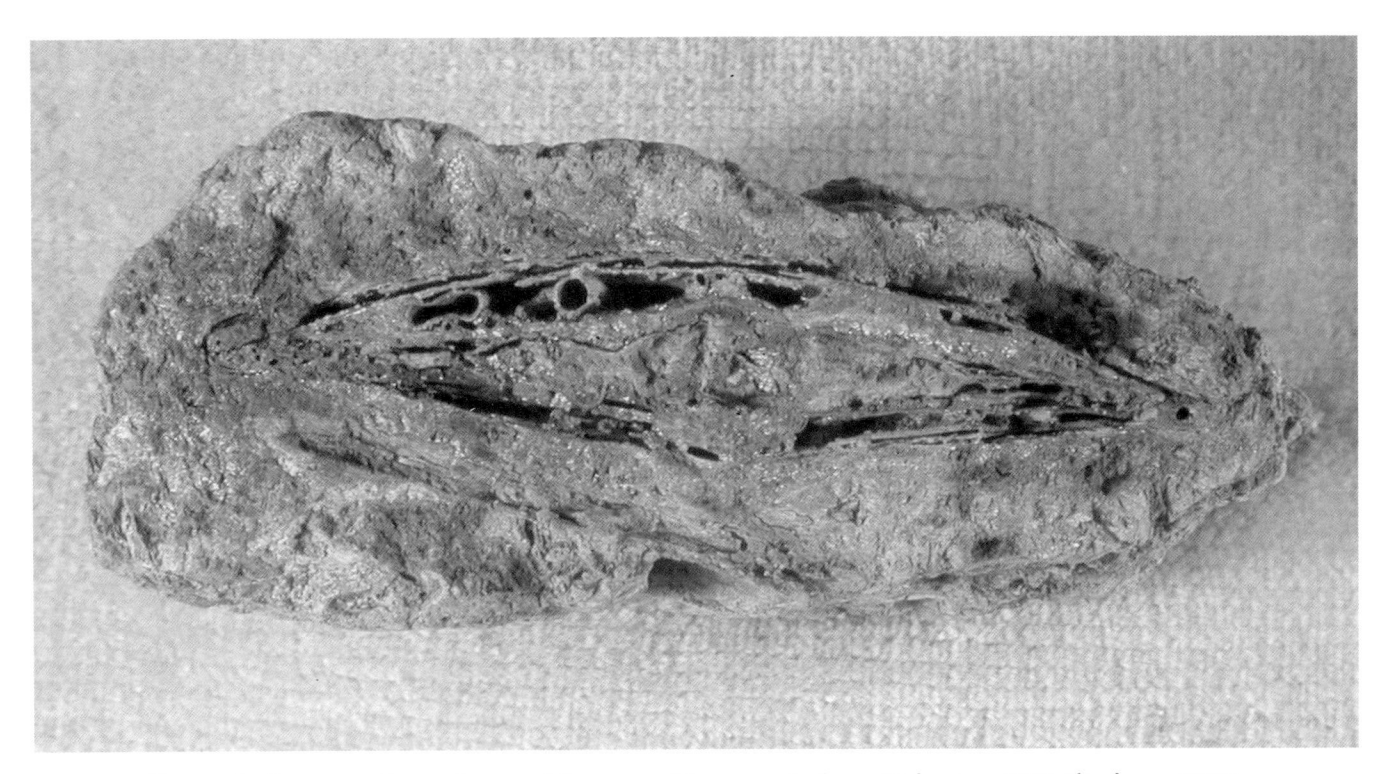

Figure 1 Cross section of one of the sword fragments from Fiskerton 1981 (find no. /222\), as received from the excavation. The section shows evidence, within the dense and obscuring layers of ferrous accretion, for what appears to be a wooden scabbard encapsulating the blade. Maximum overall dimensions of cross section - 6cms x 2.5cms.
Photo Lincolnshire County Council, Heritage Service, Conservation Department

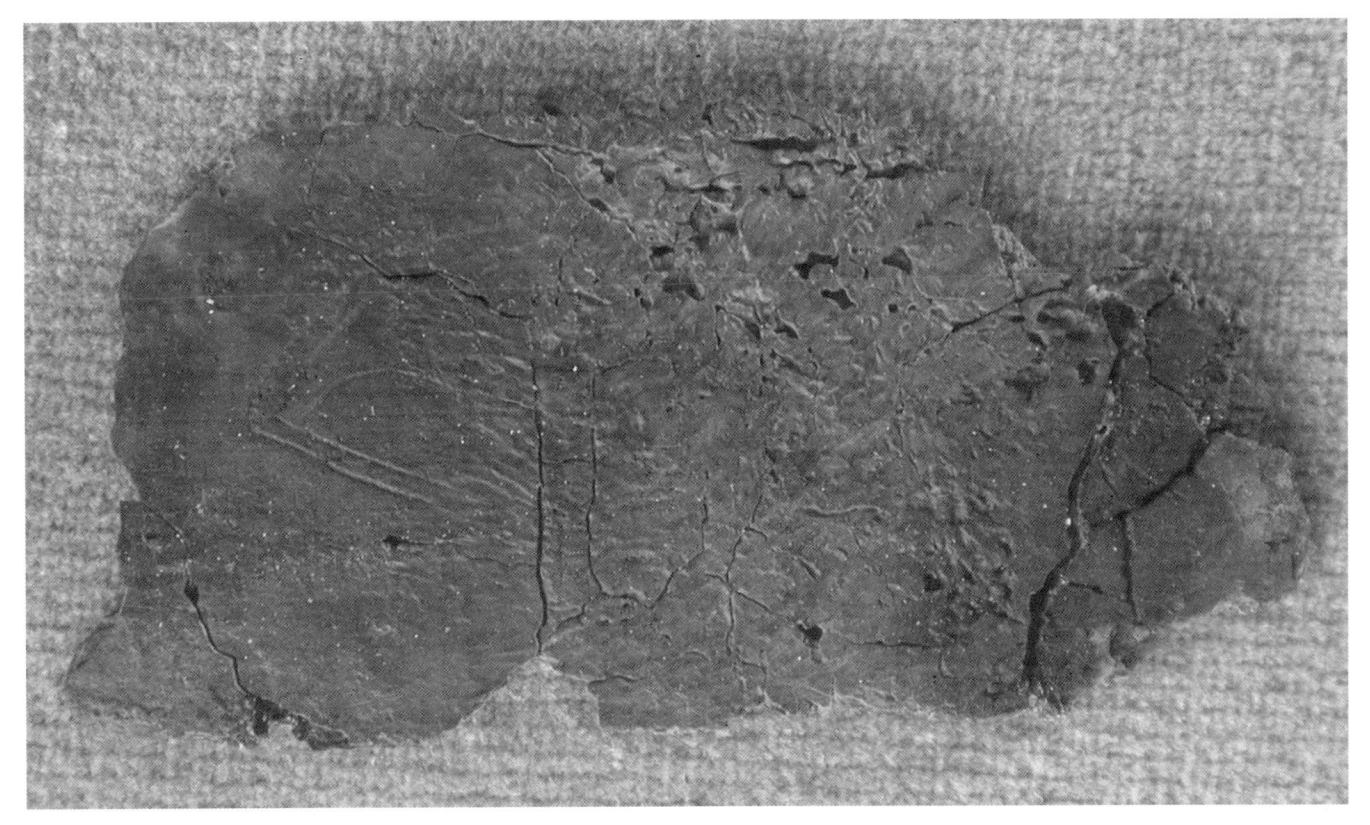

Figure 2 Small saw blade fragment (find no. /288\) from Fiskerton 1981 excavation. The fragment is in an advanced state of deterioration. Controlled removal of obscuring corrosion products has revealed evidence for surface decoration. Maximum overall dimensions of fragment - 5.7cms x 3cms.
Photo Lincolnshire County Council, Heritage Service, Conservation Department

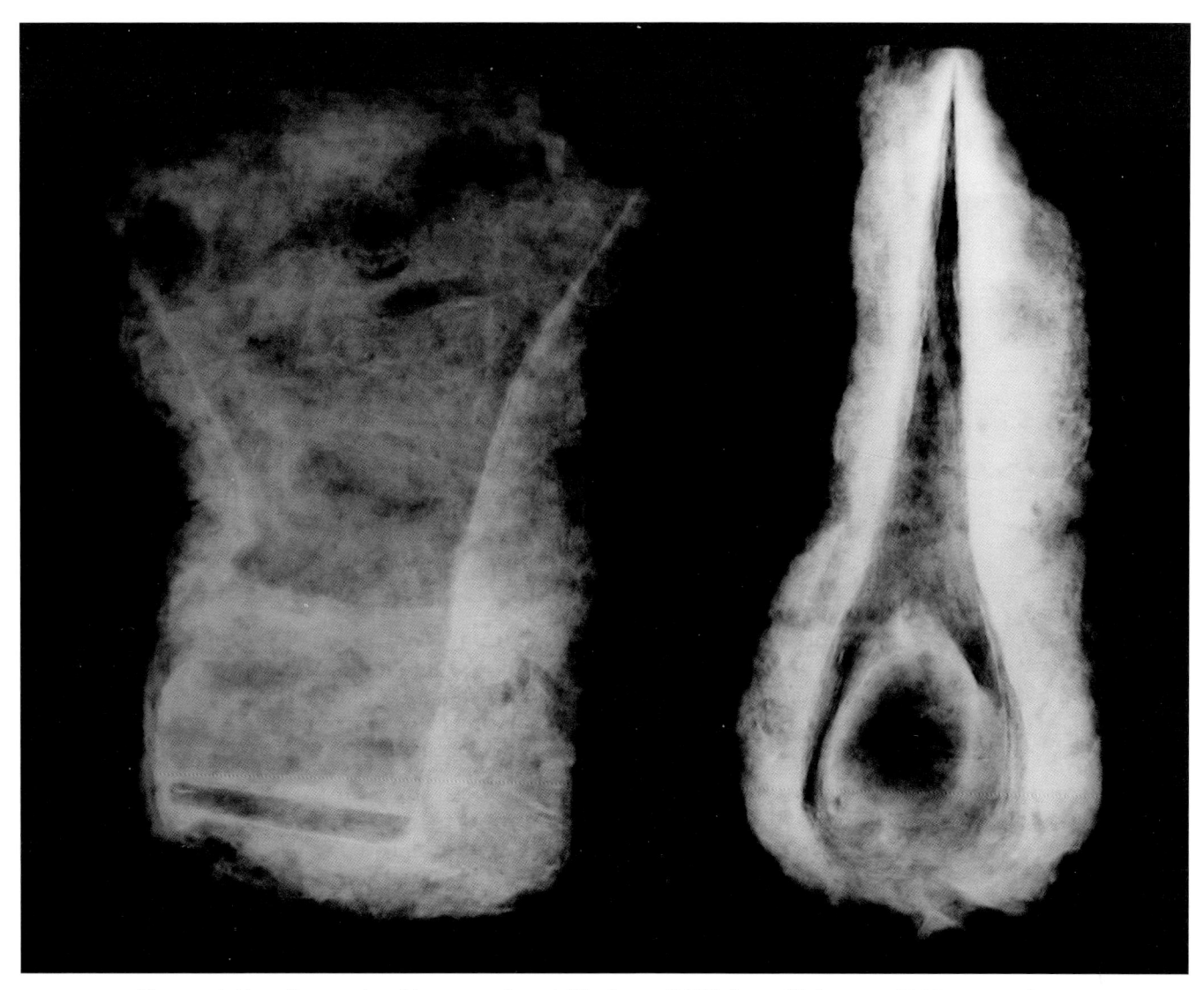

Figure 4 X-radiograph of iron axe-head (find no. /323\) from Fiskerton 1981 excavation.
(The image displays two elevations of the same object, with a ninety-degree rotation). The x-ray is
indicative of almost complete mineralisation throughout this object.
Photo Lincolnshire County Council, Heritage Service, Conservation Department

Clearly, a number of other archive enhancing analytical procedures could be applied as part of this forensic exploration. A survey of appropriate features using x-ray fluorescence spectrometry, microstructural analysis such as Fell's existing work, or perhaps even organic residue analysis to address other specific questions, are all possibilities.

In summary then, these three areas of activity,

- informed recovery,

- stabilisation of degraded structures with a balance between access and long-term integrity, and,

- examination and interpretation to inform archive reporting and subsequent assessment,

are the cornerstones of the MAP2 Conservation Strategy.

MAP2, in the spirit of PPG16 and supported by further professional documentation such as the Society of Museum Archaeologist's *Towards an Accessible Archaeological Archive: The Transfer of Archaeological Archives to Museums*, places the onus of responsibility for completion of these levels of work, on those responsible for generating the material (Owen 1995). Ensuring that these areas of responsibility are clearly recognised and understood by the various stakeholders in a project such as this, before a spade enters the earth, is crucial to its effective delivery. This in turn places a responsibility on the local curatorial constituency and the mechanisms it adopts to regulate such matters. Embedding conservation practice at the level described in those mechanisms can assist that process. At the very least the elements of work alluded to might form the basis of any discussion aimed at establishing an explicit schedule of artifact care, which contracting partners on the Witham project might have. They are generic, benchmark functions which can be applied without ambiguity, whether it be in respect of a bronze pin or a log-boat, given that they work in synergy with appropriate specialist advice and selection.

Distinct from all of this, but effectively facilitated by the delivery of these standards, are the responsibilities of the receiving organisations. These are perhaps the subject of a separate discussion, but would include the ongoing curatorial assessment and care duties related to the material, plus an increasing responsibility toward its advocacy, and for making it accessible to newer and wider audiences. A desire, by all of those involved in the project, to work together to implement robust stewardship principles will be key to ensuring the interpretation and long-term integrity of any future items or assemblages which this project might produce.

Bibliography

English Heritage, 1991, *The Management of Archaeological Projects Edition 2* (London, English Heritage).

Panter, I., 2002, 'Future Funding Sources for Conservation?', *Conservation News* No.78, UKIC Newsletter.

Fell, V. and Salter, C.J., 1998, 'Metallographic Examination of Seven Iron Age Ferrous Axeheads from England', *The Journal of the Historical Metallurgy Society*, Vol. 32, No.1.

Owen, J. (ed), 1995, *Towards An Accessible Archaeological Archive. The Transfer of Archaeological Archives to Museums, First Edition*, Society of Museum Archaeologists Occasional Paper.

SITE MANAGEMENT AND INTERPRETATION IN THE LOCAL COMMUNITY

by David Start

The Abbeys Of The Witham Valley

The archaeological potential of the Witham valley is exceptional, as is amply demonstrated throughout this volume. Perhaps the best known and most tangible features of this archaeological landscape are the monastic sites that lie along the margins of the valley. Eight on the eastern bank: Monk's Abbey, Bullington, Barlings, Stainfield, Bardney, Tupholme, Stixwould and Kirkstead, and four to the west: Nocton; Catley, Haverholme and Kyme. The sites are unusually close together (some less than 3km) clearly disregarding the monastic tendency for isolation. Indeed, the Witham valley is said to exhibit the highest density of religious houses in the country. The reasons for this abnormal clustering are thought to be the lure of the prosperity and ecclesiastical prestige of Lincoln attracting new monastic foundations, linked with the desire of the resultant monasteries to have easy access to the river Witham. The river was a busy trade link between Lincoln and the port of Boston which was at that time one of the principal ports of England. With the main income of the monasteries coming from wool production, a navigable link to the river Witham was a useful, perhaps essential, asset.

The locations of the abbey sites are shown on Fig. 1 (pg 7) of the Everson and Stocker paper (this volume). They represent a range of orders, including Augustinian, Benedictine, Cistercian, Gilbertine and Premonstratensian. Stainfield and the latter phase of Stixwould were for nuns.

The abbeys of the Witham valley have attracted much antiquarian interest since the start of the eighteenth century but have been a steadily diminishing resource until the twentieth owing to persistent recycling! When the abbeys were constructed (mostly in the mid-twelfth century) the transport of building stone down the river from quarries on the limestone escarpment around Lincoln must have been a massive undertaking. Following the Dissolution the attraction of such excellent building material, in a landscape otherwise devoid of stone, was irresistible and many farmhouses, barns and cottages around the abbey sites bear witness to its extensive re-use. John Byng, writing of Barlings in 1791, notes " what remains ... must soon come to the ground; for they are daily carting away the stones and much has fallen or been pull'd down, within these three years" (Andrews 1934). Most of the sites have some earthworks visible but only four (Barlings, Kirkstead, Kyme, and Tupholme) still exhibit standing remains.

During the eighteenth and nineteenth centuries the monastic sites in the Witham valley became a focus for curiosity and research and antiquarians and artists visited the sites and recorded the remains. Notably, William Stukeley visited in around 1716 and sketched parts of Nocton, Kirkstead and Tupholme (Stukeley 1724)(Fig. 1) and the artist and engraver, Samuel Buck, drew Barlings, Kirkstead and Tupholme, which he published in 1726 (Buck & Buck 1726, 164, 169 & 180).

Figure 1 William Stukeley published drawings of some elements of the Witham Abbeys in *Itinerarium Curiosum* produced in 1724.

The Excavation of Bardney Abbey

In February 1909 the vicar of Bardney, the Reverend Charles Laing, hired a team of labourers and began excavating on the site of Bardney Abbey. Part of the attraction of Bardney was the knowledge that there had been a Saxon monastery founded there c. 679 which became a shrine to St Oswald. The story of the arrival of the cart containing Oswald's relics is related by Bede (Colgrave & Mynors 1969) and gives rise to the Lincolnshire adage "Do you come from Bardney?" ... meaning a door has been left open (Everson this volume). The Saxon monastery was destroyed by Danish raiders around 870 and in 913 Oswald's bones were removed to Gloucester. Bardney was refounded, initially as a priory, in 1087, by Gilbert de Gant and it is the site of this post-conquest foundation that Laing began excavating in 1909. The site of the Saxon abbey is not known and there is little from Laing's excavation to suggest that it was on the site of the medieval foundation. John Leland visited Bardney shortly before its suppression in 1537 and he recorded "the monkes hold opinion that the old Abbay of Bardeney was not in the very same place wher the new ys, but at a graunge or dayre of theirs a myle of" (Smith 1964, V, 36). David Stocker has considered the location of Bardney's Saxon monastery (Stocker 1993, 107-110) and comments "the early monastery should be understood as the whole island of Bardney, within which there were many foci of which only one became the post-conquest monastery whose monks passed time with Leland". Perhaps the investigations proposed in other papers in this volume will help us understand better the location and layout of the early abbey.

Charles Laing excavated at Bardney over five years, ceasing with the outbreak of the Great War in 1914. He uncovered the lower courses and floor of the abbey church, and the cloister with chapter house, dorter, frater, abbots lodging and service rooms surrounding it, and was able to reconstruct an accurate plan of the main buildings. Laing's work, including a detailed plan of the buildings, was published in 1922 by Harold Brakspear (Brakspear 1922). For its time, the excavation of Bardney Abbey was carried out reasonably well, although it had none of the routine stratigraphic or depositional analysis that we would expect today. However, for 1909 this was pioneering work and must have encouraged much academic and popular interest. A series of 45 postcard views of the excavated remains was published while the work was in progress, giving some hint of the novelty value of the excavations (Fig. 2).

The remains of Bardney Abbey were left on view for nearly twenty years but by 1933 the effects of weathering coupled with the erosion caused by the feet of thousands of visitors were giving rise to grave concern for the future of the monument. No conservation for presentation had been carried out and the surviving masonry was deteriorating markedly. Thus, Bardney was carefully re-buried, spare stone and rubble being piled on the wall tops and covered over with soil. The effect, when all this is grassed over (and well grazed), is of a very precisely defined earthwork with all the elements of the claustral buildings easily recognisable in plan (Fig. 3). Given the difficulty of interpretation of the earthworks at other abbey sites in the Witham valley group, Bardney presents a most useful and visitable example despite the fact that it has no standing ruins.

Figure 2 One of the series of over 45 postcards produced during the excavations of Bardney Abbey in 1909 – 1914.
from the postcard collection of D.N. Robinson

Survey and Presentation

Despite Charles Laing's pioneering work at Bardney no formal excavation or survey work took place at any of the other Witham Abbey sites until the 1970s and interest waned in the monuments, and their associated historic landscapes. It was Andrew White, a particularly energetic curator at Lincoln's

Figure 3 In 1933 the excavated stonework at Bardney Abbey was reburied, leaving a very precisely defined earthwork. This aerial photograph of the excavated area of the precinct (North is to the left) shows the cruciform abbey church (with rows of columns clearly visible) adjoining the site of the cloister which is surrounded by the main monastic buildings. Photo C. Cruickshank

City and County Museum, who reawakened awareness of these, and many other sites and structures of interest in the county, in the late 1970s. White published the series *of Lincolnshire Museums Information Sheets* which included Barlings Abbey (No. 5), Tupholme Abbey (No.10) and Nocton Park Priory (No. 15) (White 1979, a, b & c). He also produced a series of four 'Guides', detailing notable features in Lincolnshire, one of which was *Abbeys of the Witham Valley between Lincoln and Tattershall* (White 1978). This leaflet included details of seven of the sites with a guided tour which added up to a 45 mile round trip. White's assertion that the tour could "form the basis of a day's outing by car or cycle" gives some hint of his enthusiasm and energy, although there is no record that he (or anyone else) ever did cycle the 45 miles and visit all the sites in one day! White's work did much to promote the heritage of Lincolnshire in general and raised public awareness of the Witham abbey sites. Others were also at work; between 1980 and 1984 the Royal Commission on the Historical Monuments of England (RCHME) undertook a meticulous survey of medieval earthworks in West Lindsey. This work, much of which was published in 1991 (Everson, Taylor & Dunn 1991) includes detailed surveys of the sites of Barlings and Stainfield and notes on Bullington Priory and Bardney Abbey.

Heritage Lincolnshire and Tupholme Abbey

The Heritage Trust of Lincolnshire was conceived in 1987, begun in 1988 and became an independent charitable trust in 1991. It was created through the efforts of Lincolnshire County Council who continue to support it. In October 1988, when we were only a few weeks into the process of creating the Trust, the site of Tupholme Abbey came on the market. Together with the then Director of the Trust, Dr Peter Hayes, I went to visit Tupholme Abbey, partly to assess its suitability to provide offices for the Trust. Absurd though that may now sound, until 1988 there had been a substantial brick and stone farmhouse on the site together with a smaller stone cottage. However, the spectacle that greeted us on that first visit soon put any thought of the re-use of redundant farm buildings out of our minds. The post-medieval buildings had been demolished, only leaving what was necessary to support the leaning monastic ruin (Figs. 4 and 5). The ruin itself was extensively vandalised and displayed a makeshift sign declaring it to be a dangerous structure. All around was strewn with demolition rubble, although it was quite clear that the demolition had taken place primarily to recover and sell the building stone which was itself originally from the abbey remains. The site was a Scheduled Ancient Monument and the post-medieval buildings were part of a grade I listed structure, but the damage had occurred despite this maximum statutory protection. The rest of the site was also in poor condition with negligible management of hedges and fences and the fishponds clearly used for dumping a variety of domestic and agricultural refuse.

Discussions with Graham Fairclough of English Heritage revealed that they also were most concerned about the damage and poor management but the company who owned the site were in liquidation and there was no easy way to

Figure 4 Tupholme Abbey farm in 1972 – The stone and brick buildings, which form an enclosed farmyard, are derelict but sturdy. Photo J. Turner

Figure 5 Tupholme Abbey in 1988 – The majority of the farm buildings have been demolished and the stone sold. Only rubble and unwanted Victorian bricks remain. Fortunately the medieval ruin, although in poor condition, was not destroyed. Photo Heritage Lincolnshire

ascertain who had carried out the demolition. As a means of establishing a better management regime for the future, English Heritage suggested that the newly formed Heritage Trust of Lincolnshire might purchase the site and manage it as an ancient monument. The field containing the remains of Tupholme is slightly less than 20 acres and was on the market at £26,000. English Heritage offered grant aid up to half of the asking price if the Trust could raise the remainder. The Trust approached both East Lindsey District Council and Lincolnshire County Council with requests for £6,000 from each, and launched a public appeal for the remaining £1,000.

Significantly, the Heritage Trust was not formally constituted at this stage, still being attached to the County Council until it gained its charitable and limited company status. Were such a proposal to be dealt with by the Trust today, the first question from the Trustees would inevitably be "where is the revenue coming from?" Not so in 1988 when Trustees had yet to be appointed. The evident needs of this dilapidated monument cried out for sensitive management and it was this that drove us on, but these days we would not begin the process of acquiring a monument until we had first established how its future management would be funded.

Management Plan

The Trust was successful in its appeals for capital funding and the site of Tupholme Abbey was purchased in December 1988. In the following weeks we drew up an initial management plan for the site, the long term aims being:

a. To protect the architectural and archaeological remains, both visible and buried.
b. To manage the wildlife … and grazing so as to enhance the heritage value of the site …
c. To equip, maintain, interpret and present the site in a way that appeals to … the widest practicable range of visitors.
d. To achieve financial viability through a combination of fund-raising activities, official grants, donations and revenue generated at the site, as well as by mobilising the enthusiasm, energy, skills and experience of voluntary supporters.

a) Architectural and archaeological remains.

The fabric of the standing ruin was clearly in a very poor state, suffering from a general lack of conservation exacerbated by vandalism. It was

Figure 6 Repairs in progress in 1990. A major element of the cost was the protective access scaffolding necessary to conserve the top of the stonework. Photo Heritage Lincolnshire

evident that parts of the arches of the high lancet windows had recently fallen. As a prime aim was to have the site freely open to the public, repairing the monument was among our first priorities. As a pre-cursor to any grant work, English Heritage grant aided a full photogrammetric survey of the medieval portion of the standing ruin. We then commissioned a condition and repair survey from Derek Latham and Associates of Derby. The first phase of repair work took place between February and June 1990 and was undertaken in partnership with the Lincoln based National Historical Building Crafts Institute (now sadly gone). The upper parts of the ruin were repaired and consolidated at a cost of £36,000 (Fig. 6). The site was officially opened to the public on 14th April 1990 while that work was still in progress (Fig. 7). Because of the need to raise additional funding of £14,000, the lower portions of the monument were not repaired until the Spring of 1993.

The site was covered in earthworks relating to the abbey buildings, the post-dissolution house and eighteenth and nineteenth century farm buildings, none of which had ever been surveyed. At the request of English Heritage, the RCHME carried out a full earthwork survey of the site coupled with aerial photographic interpretation of surviving archaeological features in the surrounding arable fields. This survey, together with the RCHME interpretation of the monument, gave us a firm basis for the planned interpretive material.

b) Managing wildlife and grazing.

Tupholme Abbey is a single field of pasture in a vast sea of arable agriculture. As such it is a haven for what wildlife there is. The Lincolnshire Wildlife Trust was consulted and site investigations were arranged with survey work being organised by Riseholme Agricultural College using and training pupils from the Queen Elizabeth Grammar School at Horncastle. The result of the surveys showed the flora and fauna to be extensive but (with the exception of a colony of great crested newts) largely unremarkable. Advice was obtained on future management of the site which had previously been let for grazing by cattle and had been regularly treated with a nitrate fertiliser and broad-leaf herbicide. The resultant pasture, whilst green and lush, was not species rich. On advice, we adopted a non-fertiliser and non-herbicide regime in the hope that, in the longer term, this would encourage a species rich flora. It was decided that the grazing should only be let for sheep as they are less damaging to earthworks than cattle. For several years the Trust grazed its own flock of Soay sheep at the site, which gave added interest for visitors, but regrettably this was discontinued in 1998 due to the difficulties of managing livestock at a distance. The grazing is now let commercially for more conventional sheep.

Since 1992 the site has been in Countryside Stewardship and the management regime has been guided by the criteria for the scheme. Hedge replanting and maintenance and hedgerow tree-planting has been included in recent years and a partnership with the British Trust for Conservation Volunteers (BTCV) has enabled weekend courses in hedge-laying to take place – a useful (if incremental) way of getting the hedges traditionally maintained.

c) Interpretation and Presentation

Initially presentation was dependent on making the site safe enough to permit visitor access. The area around the ruins was strewn with demolition rubble and general rubbish and the first priority was to remove and store or discard this material. An interim information leaflet was produced which also carried an appeal for help and/or financial contributions. The site was opened to the public with suitable pomp and ceremony on 14th April 1990 (Fig. 7), as soon as the upper portions of the ruin had been made safe. A temporary information panel (which in the event served for over three years) was provided. Despite the paucity of information concerning the layout of the monastic

Figure 7 The official opening of Tupholme Abbey on 14th April 1990. From left to right David Mountain (Chairman of the Friends of Tupholme Abbey), Mrs Hoyes, Dr Peter Hayes (Director of Heritage Lincolnshire) and Cllr Dennis Hoyes (Chairman of Lincolnshire County Council).
Photo Heritage Lincolnshire

buildings, an artist's impression of the abbey was commissioned from retired architect David Vale. In 1992 the single temporary information panel was replaced by four permanent panels and a more up to date information leaflet was published. A proposal to construct a 'Witham Abbeys Visitor Centre' within the footprint of the post-medieval farm buildings was drawn up and considered but was not followed up.

Access to the entire site was permitted, but Tupholme lay tantalisingly close to route of Lincolnshire's long distance path, the Viking Way. Footpath researchers were convinced that the track through the abbey field, which still served to link local farms, had once been a public right of way, although it was not shown as such on the definitive footpath maps. A case for reinstatement of the route as a bridle path was made in 1991 and the route was eventually (it took seven years!) adopted as a right of way making access to the Viking Way straightforward.

d) Financial viability and mobilising support

It was clear from the outset that we would need to obtain practical help and assistance in order to bring the abbey site back into good management. The task of cleaning up the site was begun with the help of officer cadets from the Royal Air Force College at Cranwell but a more sustained approach was needed. A local Councillor (Cllr Alan Bidgood) assisted the setting up of a support group which, in due course was named The Friends of Tupholme Abbey (FOTA). For the first two or three years of the project this group were crucial in the preparation of the site for opening and in its management in the early years (Figs. 8 and 9). FOTA attracted over 100 members at its height, but it was the fifteen to twenty who actively involved themselves in conservation activities who were the key to its success. This core of support carried out a wide range of tasks on the site and ran a range of fund-raising activities which contributed towards the capital costs of repair and presentation. They mobilised local schoolchildren to take an interest in the site and its wildlife and formed an informal warden service while building works were going on. It is sad to report that when the work was largely done and only very routine tasks of management and maintenance were required, the group lost its impetus and eventually disbanded. To this day, I remain pleasantly surprised at the willingness and enthusiasm with which they answered our call for help and grateful for the immense amount of effort that was expended on our behalf. To some extent this tradition lives on in our current partnership with BTCV and their weekends spent laying hedges and planting trees.

The Friends of Tupholme Abbey worked hard to raise funds for the site, and contributed to the £36,000 required for the first phase of the repairs. The funding for this work came mainly from English Heritage and the Trust's own budgets. The second phase of repairs cost £14,000 and funding was raised from English Heritage, East Lindsey District Council, the Monument Trust and the Alan Evans Memorial Trust. The challenge with managing ancient monuments is not really the capital costs for repairs and presentation, but the everyday costs of management which include regular site visits (staff time and travel costs) for checking the facilities, litter picking, and minor repairs and maintenance. Part of this requirement can be met by letting the field for grazing sheep, but even though it is nearly 20 acres, an unfertilised and 'weedy' (*i.e.* species rich!) pasture in a solidly arable area, does not attract the highest of rents. Nevertheless, the

Figures 8 & 9 Our voluntary support group, the Friends of Tupholme Abbey, were crucial to the preparation of the site for opening and in its management in the early years. Left, clearing demolition rubble from the area around the ruin; right, tackling the site's neglected hedges. Photo Heritage Lincolnshire

grazing licence is an important element of the revenue of the site. The other part, since 1992, has been the income from having the site in Countryside Stewardship. This grant-giving scheme was originally operated through the Countryside Commission, then moved to MAFF and is now with DEFRA. There are some disadvantages to being in Countryside Stewardship (e.g. the limitation on number of grazing stock) but on the whole it is an ideal scheme for the management of rural ancient monument sites. Although the grant given is small (currently £660 per year for Tupholme) together with the grazing fee, it makes routine management of the site viable.

It had been envisaged that it might be possible to let the site for events or for the Trust to run profit-making events on the site. In practice, Tupholme's remoteness and its lack of basic resources such as electricity or toilet facilities has limited this opportunity. The site has been let on occasions for Caravan Club or equestrian events but such opportunities are rare. In 1999 the Trust organised an ambitious music festival at the site (with historical justification as Tupholme was notoriously the site of the ill-famed Bardney Pop Festival of 1972 – see Cope-Faulkner and Lane, 1999) but despite attracting over 1500 people, the festival was not a financial success. Arguably it was a success if we consider that it attracted 1500 people to an ancient monument who might not otherwise have chosen to visit it!

Future Management

The success of the first ten years under the Countryside Stewardship Scheme, not only in providing a source of revenue for the site, but also in protecting and enhancing the natural heritage of the Abbey, has been encouraging. 2003 marks the first year of a new Countryside Stewardship Agreement at Tupholme, which will run until 2013. We are endeavouring to improve the visitor facilities and the Trust has recently been awarded funding from the landfill tax rebate scheme and British Sugar to undertake a project to enhance public access to the site. This will include a pedestrian bridge spanning the water-filled moat around the picnic area and way-markers that will lead visitors around the site and enable them to see more of its features. The project is to be carried out by the BTCV and we hope that local volunteers might also be inspired to rekindle their interest and involvement with the site. Further events are planned at the Abbey to encourage more visitors and allow them to engage with and enjoy their local heritage.

Interpretation and Presentation At Other Witham Abbey Sites

The Trust's involvement with Tupholme Abbey led it to develop a programme of interpretation at some of the other monastic sites.

- **Bardney:** The excavated area of Bardney Abbey had been purchased by public subscription at the time of Charles Laing's excavations. The site had been proposed for guardianship by the Ministry of Works, but had narrowly missed achieving that status and had been passed to a local charity, the Jews' Court Trust. At the time that Tupholme was being brought into new management, the Jews' Court Trust were not actively managing the site of Bardney Abbey, which was let for grazing, but had no on-site interpretation or information leaflet. The Jews' Court Trust indicated they would be agreeable to Heritage Lincolnshire undertaking a fund raising exercise to provide information panels on the site and an information leaflet to be made available locally and through Tourist Information Centres. The Jews' Court Trust could offer some funding as they held the remaining financial balances from the 'Friends of Bardney Abbey', a support organisation which had dwindled some years ago. The other parties who made up the Bardney funding package were West Lindsey District Council, the Countryside Commission and the local agrochemical company Omex Agricultural Ltd. Two lectern-style panels were erected on the site (Fig. 10) and an

Figure 10 The information panels at Bardney Abbey (in use). Photo Heritage Lincolnshire

introductory panel was provided in a small car park which was created close to the entrance gate for the site. The land for the small three-car car park was loaned by the farmer of the surrounding fields, through whose farmyard visitors to Bardney Abbey have to drive. The farmer was of the opinion that he would rather formalise visitor behaviour by providing a car park than have people wandering around the farmyard and parking randomly. He also felt it was better for his security – cars parking in the abbey car park were clearly stating the proposed intentions of their inhabitants and the farmer felt comfortable about their presence on his land.

The original interpretive panels were fitted in 1992 and by 1999 the lectern style panels had faded quite markedly due to sunlight. Two replacement panels were recently commissioned by the Jews' Court Trust, funded by a landfill tax grant.

- **Barlings:** The site at Barlings has an impressive standing ruin and although it is on private land it has a public footpath running through the main area of earthworks. However, access to the footpath and the site was somewhat daunting as the path ran through working livery stables. We negotiated for an improved access to the site with a permissive path to the ruins. This involved the provision of some new fencing and gates and the construction of steps, which was carried out by the British Trust for Conservation Volunteers. In addition we persuaded the farmer to enter a Countryside Stewardship agreement which helped with funding towards the two interpretive panels on the site and gave enhanced access around the perimeter of the site, allowing good views of the fishponds. An information leaflet was also produced. The funding package was complex and comprised West Lindsey District Council, The Rural Development Commission, the Countryside Commission, Omex Agriculture Ltd, and the J W Wright Trust. The limited space available at Barlings allowed no room for any car parking, although a slight widening of the verge was carried out. We have always been wary of encouraging too much vehicular traffic to Barlings Abbey as the road is single track and there is very limited space for visitors' cars.

- **Kirkstead:** In the early 1990s the Kirkstead Abbey site was owned by Nottingham University. Initial discussions with the University encouraged us to think that we might persuade them to allow the provision of some information panels for visitors to the site. As a preliminary, we asked the RCHME if it would be possible for an earthwork survey of the site to be carried out and this was done in 1993. However, Nottingham University then decided to sell Kirkstead Abbey and the new owners were not inclined to encourage public access to the site. Kirkstead is a very visitable site with an imposing ruin and excellent earthworks. There is visitor access across the site, via a trackway through the earthworks which leads to the nearby church of St Leonard's (which is associated with the Abbey) but the owners prefer visitors not to stray from the path. We are hopeful that they might review this policy in the future.

- **Catley:** The site of Catley Priory is owned by Lincolnshire County Council (LCC) and let to a local farmer. Permissive access to the site was arranged in 1991 and the site was included in the North Kesteven Medieval Trail, compiled by the Heritage Trust in that year (NKDC 1991). In 1998/99 the Trust developed a Heritage Lottery bid for North Kesteven District Council, for the provision of improved access, car parking facilities and information panels at the major sites on the Medieval Trail.

At Catley Priory this initiative sparked a partnership exercise between Lincolnshire County Council and the Heritage Trust. The County Council were already reviewing the management of the site, which at that time was half under pasture with the other half in arable and regularly ploughed. The County Archaeologist successfully negotiated with the LCC property department and the tenant farmer, to cease ploughing the scheduled area. The tenant was then persuaded to enter a stewardship agreement to put the whole monument, including the non-scheduled areas under grass and to accommodate improved visitor facilities. Public access to the entire monument is now available. Before this change took place, the County Archaeologist commissioned an earthwork survey, a geophysical survey and detailed fieldwalking of the ploughed portion. The on-site information panels were provided through the HLF project and enhanced by LCC's provision of a four-bay car-park and a landscaped area which it is proposed to developed as a picnic area. The County Council own several other

scheduled monuments and Catley Priory has served as an excellent model for positive management which will be used when reviewing the management of their other sites.
- **South Kyme:** The fabric of St Mary and All Saints, the parish church of South Kyme, is largely based on the west end of the south aisle of the priory church, with Victorian alterations by C. H. Fowler. One can thus argue that South Kyme presents the largest standing portion of any of the Witham abbeys, although all other traces of the site are lost under ploughed fields. The church, and the nearby fourteenth century tower which once formed part of Sir Gilbert de Umfraville's grand house are featured in The Medieval Trail (Orr, no date) and have an on-site information panel.

During the past fifteen years, much has been achieved in the process of negotiating access to, and providing information about, the sites of the Witham Abbeys. The work has entailed many partnerships involving the Heritage Trust of Lincolnshire, Lincolnshire County Council, the District Councils of East and West Lindsey and North Kesteven, English Heritage, the Friends of Tupholme Abbey and the British Trust for Conservation Volunteers. Funding has been obtained from a very wide range of sources including local authorities, national agencies charitable Trusts, local companies and support groups. One of the most important elements throughout has been the enthusiasm of members of the public to help out in many practical ways. The wholehearted involvement of local people in this work has been an extremely rewarding factor for the heritage professionals working on the project and has also helped develop a sense of participation in, and ownership of, their heritage for the members of the public who have taken part in the work.

Bibliography

Andrews, C. B., ed., 1934, *The Torrington Diaries. A tour through England and Wales of the Hon. John Byng 1781 - 1794*. 4 vols (London, Eyre Spottiswood).

Brakspear, S.A.J., 1922, Bardney Abbey, *Archaeol J*, 79, 1-92.

Colgrave, B. and Mynors, R.A.B., 1969, *Bede's Ecclesiastical History of the English People* (Oxford).

Cope-Faulkner, P. and Lane, T., 1999, *The Nice People Are Here, Pop Festivals in Lincolnshire* (Heckington, Heritage Trust of Lincolnshire).

Everson, P.L., Taylor, C.C. and Dunn, C.J., 1991, *Change and Continuity - Rural Settlement in North-West Lincolnshire* (London, HMSO).

N.K.D.C., 1991, *The Medieval Trail A Journey Through North Kesteven in the Middle Ages* (Sleaford, North Kesteven District Council).

Orr, K., no date, *The Medieval Trail A Journey Through North Kesteven in the Middle Ages* (Sleaford, North Kesteven District Council and Heritage Trust of Lincolnshire).

Figure 11 The site of Tupholme Abbey is one of the few Witham Abbey sites with standing remains. The whole of one wall of the refectory survives with a pulpit built into the wall thickness on the upper floor.
Photo Heritage Lincolnshire

Stocker, D., 1993, 'The Early Church in Lincolnshire: A Study of the Sites and their Significance', in Vince, A.G. (ed), *Pre-Viking Lindsey*, Lincoln Archaeological Studies 1, (Lincoln, CLAU).

Stukeley, W., 1724, *Itinerarium Curiosum* (1st edition).

Smith, L.T., (ed), 1964, *Leland's itinerary in England and Wales* (Five Volumes).

White, A.J., 1979a, *Barlings Abbey*, Lincolnshire Museums Information Sheet, Archaeology Series 5 (Lincoln).

White, A.J., 1979b, *Tupholme Abbey*, Lincolnshire Museums Information Sheet, Archaeology Series 10 (Lincoln).

White, A.J., 1979c, *Nocton Park Priory*, Lincolnshire Museums Information Sheet, Archaeology Series 15 (Lincoln).

White, A.J., 1978, *Abbeys of the Witham Valley between Lincoln and Tattershall*, Lincolnshire Museums Guide (Lincoln).

PRESENTATION TO THE WIDER WORLD

by Thomas Cadbury

This paper examines the role of museums in the construction and dissemination of knowledge about the archaeology of the Witham valley. It focusses in particular on the City and County Museum that, since 1906, has held Lincolnshire's major archaeological collections. In 2005 a new City and County Museum will open to the public, marking a major event for the interpretation of Lincolnshire's heritage. This paper discusses the issues and opportunities that this new museum will bring to the interpretation of the Witham valley and highlights the importance that a local museum working with partners can play in such a role.

Museums are a physical manifestation of a public fascination with the past, or to put it in the words of the Museums' Association mission statement 'Museums enable people to explore collections for inspiration and enjoyment' (Museums' Association 2002). For archaeology museums and their collections this manifests itself as a concern to collect and preserve the material culture of the past and the construction of meaning from them for the present. The history of this concern in Lincolnshire can be seen to be much older than the lifetime of today's museums. In particular a concern with the past of the Witham valley seems to have a long history. Medieval readings of symbolic meaning in the Witham valley landscape relating to much earlier traditions are suggested by Stocker and Everson (2002). They present the evidence for a tradition of votive deposition stretching from the late Bronze Age through to the medieval period. This tradition seems to be associated with causeways crossing the Witham which existed prior to the medieval period and may all have prehistoric origins. Stocker and Everson conclude that on the arrival of Christianity an earlier meaningful symbolic landscape was 'converted' and given new meanings.

Many of the finds of votive objects were made during the scouring, straightening and embanking of the river in the eighteenth and nineteenth centuries. These operations brought up large quantities of metal artefacts of prehistoric to medieval date. The antiquarian collectors of the time were eager and able to obtain many of these artefacts. Joseph Banks, the President of the Royal Society, was one such collector and he acquired many such artefacts in 1788 after the publication of a notice in the Stamford Mercury:

'Any gentleman possessed of ancient weapons, utensils, or other things, found in clearing the river Witham, or elsewhere in Lincolnshire will much oblige Sir Joseph Banks by permitting him to inspect them; and he will be very thankful for any information on the subject he shall receive by post, directed to him at Revesby Abbey, near Boston.'

Banks built up a collection of Witham artefacts; he seems to have been interested in studying and classifying them much as he did for botanical and geological samples. His search for meaning from the Witham artefacts can be seen from the submission of a number of them for metallurgical testing by Dr George Pearson in 1796. Although the outcome of these tests may have been the complete destruction of the artefacts, it does illustrate the interest in scientific analysis that was forming at the time. In the 1790s items from the Banks collection were transferred to the care of the Dean and Chapter of Lincoln Cathedral. In 1810 Adam Stark describes them as being in the east end of the library over the North Cloister. It is hard to know how far public access to this material was possible while it was in the Cathedral; it is likely that it was confined to scholars. The decision to transfer the collection to the City and County Museum on its foundation in 1906 saw a conscious move to far wider public access.

The City and County Museum was founded, in part, as a move to try to preserve some of the County's archaeological discoveries in Lincoln. Many of the archaeological discoveries of the eighteenth and nineteenth centuries had found homes outside the County and there was a worry that this trend would accelerate without a museum in Lincoln. A suitable home for the museum was found in Lincoln at Greyfriars. This thirteenth century Franciscan friary building was vacant after a history of diverse use such as gunpowder store, Jersey school, Mechanics' Institute and part of the Grammar School. The collections of the Dean and Chapter, Mechanics' Institute Museum and the Lincolnshire Naturalist Union were transferred to the new museum. These collections including the finds from the Witham form a nucleus of the City and County Museum's archaeology collections. As the collections have grown they have continued to feature new finds from the Witham. One of the most prominent, and at 24 feet long certainly the largest, was a prehistoric dug-out wooden canoe found at Fiskerton Short

Figure 1 Late Bronze Age dug-out canoe, found at Short Ferry, Fiskerton.
Photo City and County Museum Lincolnshire County Council

Ferry in 1952 (Fig. 1). Other finds include further prehistoric metal tools and weapons, stone axes, medieval pottery and most recently the finds from Fiskerton 1981 (Field 1986) and 2001 (Field *et al.* this volume). In 1998 Lincolnshire County Council Heritage Services (LCCHS) was restructured, and formulated a comprehensive collections management and conservation policy (LCCHS 1999). These policies enable the needs of the collections to be identified and resources targeted to meet these needs. With large numbers of archaeological project archives entering the collections as part of the planning development process it is vital that these strategies are in place. The City and County Museum is now in a good position to care for and make accessible such collections.

The stature of the Witham finds within the Museum's collections can be seen by their prominence in displays and publications (Smith 1908, Moore 1972, White 1978, 1979 a, b, c). Since 1996 the Greyfriars Exhibition Centre (as it has come to be known) has hosted an annual temporary exhibition sourced largely from the City and County Museum collections; these exhibitions have featured many Witham finds. The City and County Museum has also produced exhibitions that have toured other Lincolnshire County Council Heritage Sites. One such exhibition was titled 'Finds from the Witham'; this used the Witham finds as a basis for a chronological exploration of the history Lincolnshire as it affected the Witham valley. With a new City and County Museum due to open to the public in 2005 the displays in Greyfriars will soon be replaced. For nearly 100 years Greyfriars and its displays will have been one of the main public expressions of archaeology in Lincolnshire; throughout that time finds from the Witham have held a central place. The dug-out canoe and metalwork finds in particular have received an almost iconic status. These objects are, in the context of the City and County Museum's collections, relatively large and complete objects; their bold shape makes them fairly accessible to visitors as dramatic symbols of the past. Witham objects such as swords, axes, spears, shields, stirrups, keys and the boat are recognisable as such. The main interpretative use of these objects was to illustrate broad themes such as chronology and artistic style. This form of interpretation has its roots in the antiquarian concern with classification and categorisation. The usual style of exhibitions in Greyfriars was a collection of glass cabinets containing objects often themed around a chronological period. This style suited the display of antiquarian finds and single casual finds that as we have seen historically made up a significant proportion of the City and County Museum's collections. Few of the finds from more recent archaeological fieldwork have been displayed in Greyfriars, this is largely due to the huge amount of conservation work that would be necessary to display such complex and sensitive material in the building's environment. Who, what, why, when and how are the classic questions posed in museum exhibition; for the Witham valley material these questions have so far only been partially examined. More attention is required in future to both individual objects and their Witham valley context.

The new City and County Museum represents an amazing opportunity to develop the public interpretation of Lincolnshire's archaeology beyond that which was possible in Greyfriars. The new museum will seek to meet the public expectations of what a museum should provide. These expectations have grown immensely; they include increased access to collections, displays that are inspiring and enjoyable, and facilities such as a café, shop and toilets. One of the main drawbacks to Greyfriars was a lack of accessible space. Greyfriars has roughly 400m^2 of public space, split half into exhibition space and half into education space with the latter only accessible by two flights of steps. The new museum will have roughly 1000m^2 of exhibition space, 350m^2 of education, an audio-visual theatre and impressive areas of circulation space all with easy access. Greyfriars has a museum shop but cannot offer visitors either refreshments or toilets. The new museum will feature a café/restaurant, shop, toilets and cloakroom facilities. All of these facilities will be backed up by behind-the-scenes services such as offices, workshops and exhibition handling facilities to Government Indemnity standard. The type of object that could be exhibited in Greyfriars was somewhat constrained by the environment in the building. The new museum's exhibition areas will be environmentally controlled thus facilitating the display of any material from the collections. For the first time the whole range of finds from the Witham valley could be displayed.

With the new building the challenge will be to ensure that all the above facilities are present and that they work both individually and collectively as a building. The building also needs to have sufficient character to make a visit a memorable experience; this is a quality that Greyfriars has in abundance. The architects for the project, Panter-Hudspith, have designed a building that is both strikingly contemporary and yet uses a design language that is sympathetic to its surroundings. It mixes materials such as concrete and stainless steel with limestone and timber. Its appearance will be both modernist and also full of the changes in angle and surface that can be seen in the urban landscape of Lincoln (Fig. 2). Inside, the public spaces must meet a high specification, be flexible enough to respond to changes in use throughout the lifetime of the building, inspire the visitor and make their visit special. The new museum will feature Education Rooms with superb views up the hillside to Lincoln Cathedral and the Orientation Hall flooded with natural light illuminating the stonework of the majestic wall to the main galleries (Fig. 3).

I hope the move from Greyfriars to the new building will have a profound effect on a visitor's perception of the displays of archaeological objects. The interaction between the visitor and

Figure 2 Architects model of the new City and County Museum (seen from the North).
Photo Panter-Hudspith Architects

the object must be central to the museum experience. The increased space and accessibility, new facilities and the ability to display all types of finds should all contribute to making a visit to the museum a superb experience. The archaeology of the Witham valley provides an ideal case study for exploring the issues surrounding interpretation of such material within a museum.

The staff of the new City and County Museum are keen to interpret the Witham valley for a wide public audience. The new building represents a significant opportunity for high quality interpretation of the Witham valley. Its location, within easy access of the valley itself, is a great advantage. It is also in a an ideal position to develop good links to the local communities; the museum and its partners are busily engaged in doing this. For the interpretation and dissemination of knowledge to be successful it will be necessary to be able to respond to the changing needs of these communities, further raising the importance of developing such partnerships. The museum will function at its best as part of a network of interpretative opportunities.

The archaeology of the Witham valley can be built up from many elements: finds from archaeological fieldwork; the built environment; the natural environment; artworks and the voices of Witham communities past and present. The museum has traditionally had its most direct relationship with the finds, some of which have been in its keeping for nearly 100 years. Through this direct relationship we are in a good position to use this material for interpretation, however, we recognise the need to incorporate the other sources of evidence in order to give a full picture. A wide range of interpretative techniques will have to be explored to find the most suitable combination.

There will be potential within the new displays to look at the finds both as individual objects and as part of a bigger picture. As individual objects, the range of Witham valley finds provide the opportunity to explore such topics as technology, style and value *etc*. Many of these objects have led fascinating lives from which we can tell stories about production, use, ownership, loss, deposition, recovery, collection, conservation and display. These stories start to give us the connections to the people associated with the objects and as we start to move towards these people we are also starting to create landscapes. These landscapes can be special and topographical or they can be social, cultural or chronological.

Figure 3 Artist's impression of the Orientation Hall in the new City and County Museum.
Photo Panter-Hudspith Architects

The museum is a good environment in which to view an individual object. The object can be isolated through the use of a display case, a plinth, or by lighting through which the visitor's attention is focussed and directed. At this point interpretative techniques can be employed; the visitors' senses can be engaged through sight, touch, sound and smell. They can interact with the objects through activities or questions; graphics, text and audio-visual clips which can convey information and provide background. There will certainly be room in the new displays for such individual treatment of artefacts and many of the Witham valley objects would benefit from this approach. It is likely, however, that an even greater emphasis will be placed on the construction of a sense of place and a sense of time using groups of objects. In the case of the Witham valley there are strong groups of objects such as the Fiskerton 1981 and 2001 finds, the wider group of votive depositions and the Lincoln waterside assemblages. These groupings can tell us stories about belief and memory, about technology and craftsmanship, change and continuity and about individuals and their place within a society. These stories are the basis for the creation of landscapes and these are landscapes that need to exist outside as well as inside the museum. The museum cannot create ecosystems, grow reed-beds or manage watertables; these are best done by other bodies but the more these museum landscapes can be linked with standing monuments or reconstructed or preserved environments in the Witham valley the more effective they will be. The museum is keen to tell stories about process, about archaeological and environmental research. We need to be able to answer visitors' questions about how we construct these stories. How do we know about these peoples, what are the latest discoveries and what are we doing to find out more? The museum will have to be flexible enough to respond to change and to communicate the layers of meaning and conflicting interpretations.

The museum and its partners will have to develop effective dialogues so that projects can inform and feed each other. The ability for a visitor to be able to see the archaeology of the Witham valley and learn about the peoples who created it, before exploring the area, should certainly help bring the past to life. Some of the most exciting dialogues will be with the communities of the Witham valley today. The museum is already involved in forming links with communities and it is to be hoped that these can be extended to bring in other partners and projects as they develop. The museum has dedicated spaces for community use and the necessary staff and other resources to involve local communities in the work the museum. The value of the archaeology of the Witham valley can be promoted by interpretation, education and outreach projects. It is envisaged that a strong local museum working in partnership with others will act as a channel to continue the collective memory of the Witham valley.

Bibliography

Field, F.N., 1986, 'An Iron Age timber causeway at Fiskerton, Lincolnshire', *Fenland Research* 3, 49-53.

Lincolnshire County Council Heritage Services, 1999, *Collections Management Policy*.

Moore, C.N., 1972, *City and County Museum, Lincoln*.

Museums' Association, 2002, *Code of Ethics for Museums*.

Smith, A., 1908, *Lincoln City and County Museum Publications No. 4, Report and General Guide*.

Stocker, D. and Everson, P., 2002, 'The Straight and Narrow Way – Fenland Causeways and the Conversion of the Landscape in the Witham Valley, Lincolnshire' in Carver, M. (ed) *The Cross goes North. Processes of Conversion in Northern Europe, AD 300-1300*, (Woodbridge) 271-288.

White, A.J., 1978, *Dug-out boats from Lincolnshire and South Humberside*, Lincolnshire Museums Information Sheet, Archaeology Series 3 (Lincoln).

White, A.J., 1979a, *Antiquities from the River Witham, Part 1 Prehistoric and Roman*. Lincolnshire Museums Information Sheet, Archaeology Series 12 (Lincoln).

White, A.J., 1979b, *Antiquities from the River Witham, Part 2 Anglo-Saxon and Viking*. Lincolnshire Museums Information Sheet, Archaeology Series 13 (Lincoln).

White, A.J., 1979c, *Antiquities from the River Witham, Part 3 Medieval*. Lincolnshire Museums Information Sheet, Archaeology Series 14 (Lincoln).

THE ARCHAEOLOGY OF THE WITHAM VALLEY: SOMETHING *HAS* TO BE DONE

by Francis Pryor

This volume marks the conclusion of the first significant stage of modern research into the archaeology of the Witham valley. In current development control terminology, this report contains the desk-based assessment and the first stages of evaluation by excavation and survey. So we are now in a position to stand back, draw breath and think where next we must turn our attention. It will not be an easy matter, but I do not think that it is an option to turn our backs on the Witham valley: the archaeological and environmental deposits are there; their quality is unrivalled and their long-term future, like most fragile waterlogged and semi-waterlogged material, is by no means certain. Something *has* to be done.

It would be very tempting to use the opportunity provided by the concluding chapter of a book such as this to lay down a series of carefully defined research agenda. I do not, however, think it would necessarily be a good idea. To me it smacks of committee-based archaeology which in my experience seldom produces surprises or originality – surely the hallmarks of good research. Instead I would rather see ideas for future research spring from the bottom-up: from the teams running individual projects. The Witham Valley Archaeology Research Committee's (WVARC) role is then to ensure that the various projects taking place in the area work to common standards of data recovery and methodology, and avoid duplication of effort. As time passes, more general themes will begin to emerge. Indeed, some already have: it would be difficult to ignore the diachronic (time-depth) importance of the valley's spatial organisation, as many authors have made clear. That, however, is just one theme and there are many others that are beginning to appear. Having recognised that, I shall withdraw because it can often be counter-productive to define an idea before it becomes fully fledged. As I write I am conscious that it is spring and that fledglings can often hit the ground with a smack.

Recently the tendency has been towards more heavy-handed, top-down approaches to research. I also think it instructive that many of these large-scale projects have taken a very long time indeed to see publication; of course late publication is generally speaking irrelevant publication. I would, therefore, prefer to see our work take place within a less cumbersome, more *laissez-faire* environment, where specific research objectives remain flexible and are determined by the archaeologists at the 'coal face'. It still works well for numerous university field projects and it worked well in the 1970s, when I excavated at Fengate for the Nene Valley Research Committee. I can see no reason why this success cannot be repeated for the Witham valley. I should also add that it is already in *de facto* operation and is running very smoothly, a process helped enormously by the encouragement and academic rigour provided by Steve Catney and Jim Bonnor's Development Control teams.

Bonnor and Catney see linear development schemes – roads, pipelines, river works *etc.* – as a major archaeological impact; these, however, are schemes which by their nature traverse large tracts of landscape and can be used to co-ordinate and unite different geographical micro-regions. In their paper they also draw attention to the management tools available to them but they point out that 'the weaknesses of the… process lie in its reactivity and the lack of enforcement in the controls of permitted development.' The latter may or may not be addressed in current DCMS-led discussions over Heritage Protection Legislation Reform – discussions which will lead to a White Paper early in 2004. The former will be addressed by having regular meetings, seminars and discussions under the auspices of WVARC and others. Discussions firmly based around specific matters of substance are always more effective and to the point than meetings where various interest groups attempt to conjure research agenda 'from thin air'.

One means of clarifying one's thinking about what needs to be protected and/or preserved is to work for English Heritage's Monuments Protection Programme, like Dave Went. Dave's paper clearly demonstrates the richness and diversity of surviving sites and monuments, but it also clearly shows that they all form part of a unified whole. In other words, they require to be considered on something much wider than a simple site-by-site basis.

Having touched-on the contribution by one of our editors, Steve Catney, I will now turn to (or on?) Dave Start. Any bottom-up approach to research will benefit enormously from public involvement - ideally while it is still taking place. I have experienced such as-it-happens involvement in my own research around the Fens, and I greatly prefer it to the recent pattern of so-called involvement which could be characterised as: 'tell them about it when it's all over'. This type of Public Non-Relations will often include a slick, glossy publication, which usually verges on the patronising; such public 'involvement' tends to be associated with the larger, top-down style of project. In my experience the feed-back one gets from local people while the project is under way can have a very direct bearing on the direction research can take. Public involvement can no longer be seen as an optional add-on. It is both an essential and integral part of the process and with the joint assistance of Dave Start and WVARC it can, and must, play a significant role in the project. I should also add that it can also be great fun.

Important research must be given long-term museum and on-site display and the papers by Dave Start and Thomas Cadbury show that Lincolnshire is in the forefront here. Nowadays public access means more than just superficial inspection. People want to become involved with what they quite rightly see as *their* past. This requires imagination on the part of those who provide the displays and information panels. Having read their contributions I am now convinced that the teams available to the WVARC are more than fit for the task

Having made much of a bottom-up, flexible approach to our research I should perhaps make one important exception, which is of course palaeoenvironmental. Charly French and James Rackham make a cogent case for a valley-wide, integrated palaeoenvironmental research design. They particularly highlight the need for close co-operation between various commercially-funded projects and outline a series of steps that will help to knit-together the different parts and aspects of the region's past micro-environments. This work can usefully be co-ordinated by the existing Development Control mechanisms, but there is a pressing need for an even greater degree of integration which could be provided by a new English Heritage-funded research project. As I know from my own teams' work, which benefited enormously from Charly's researches, archaeological research in a region as diverse and low-lying as the Witham valley has to be accommodated within a reliable and all-enveloping scheme of palaeoenvironmental development. The successive changes of the various past environments of the region provide the context for human interaction. They are the canvas without which the picture cannot painted.

This book began with a short discussion of the problem posed by the archaeology of the Witham valley to people who have actually to operate there. It is only too easy as archaeologists to put the needs of antiquity first, but as Andrew Usborne of the Environment Agency stated, the Agency's main role is 'to provide improved flood protection for the people of Lincolnshire'; everything else, although plainly important, has to be of secondary importance. This work has and will involve an extensive programme of bank strengthening, during which archaeological remains are bound to be revealed, as indeed they were in 2001.

Naomi Field's excavation of the now nationally famous Fiskerton Iron Age causeway took place in 1981, following its discovery by the metal detectorist, Vernon Stuffins (searching on his mother's land), the previous year. The finds from Naomi's excavations were superb – only matched by those found in 2001. But fine finds only remain fine if they are properly conserved and the members of the WVARC are very fortunate in being able to draw upon the expertise of Rob White's County Council Conservation Laboratory in Lincoln. Rob and his team have done a superb job on the material from Jim Rylatt's recent excavation, as his paper so clearly demonstrates. Having said that, confidence in one's conservators is all-important. No matter how professional we become, I defy any archaeologist not to treat his or her best finds as something very special. I have visited Rob's laboratory and my confidence in his team is fully inspired.

The momentous discovery by Vernon Stuffins in 1980 surely has to be one of the best examples of public involvement in an archaeological project. Naomi's excavations were followed by those of Jim Rylatt some twenty years later. By now Mike Parker Pearson, of Sheffield University, was also involved and their joint paper is a fine summary of the project. Mike and colleagues at Sheffield introduced an entirely new idea – that of repairs to the timbers of the causeway on a cycle that could be linked to total lunar eclipses. This new information was based on accurate dendro-chronological dates provided by the English Heritage tree-ring laboratory at Sheffield University. If we take the high quality of finds found by Stuffins, Naomi Field and Jim Rylatt and combine them with this new information then there can be next to no doubt that the causeway played an important ritual or ceremonial role. But was that all there was to it? I think not, because it was also a real causeway, and a boundary too. Instead, perhaps we should view the Fiskerton causeway – and indeed others in the Witham Valley and further afield – as examples of what Richard Bradley has termed 'ritualisation' (Bradley, forthcoming). Ritualisation – the incorporation of ritual into important aspects of prehistoric life – seems to have been all-pervasive; it may have begun in the Bronze Age, although I would personally favour an origin prior to the Neolithic. The important point to note is that the distinction between day-to-day domestic and ritual or religious life – something which we take for granted today – simply did not exist. So perhaps the answer to the question: was Fiskerton a ritual site?, is 'sometimes'. In other words it was 'ritual', when the people using is were thinking in that way: perhaps on moonless nights, or when the wind was from the north-east, or when the time came to commemorate a long-lost, or recently departed relative.

If we embed the idea of ritualisation deep within the fabric of prehistoric society it perhaps becomes easier to account for the longevity of, for example, boundaries within the landscape. We know that life in the countryside of Roman Britain continued much as before, if only because Iron Age fields and other features frequently become absorbed into Romano-British landscapes. Of course there were profound changes – particularly as regards the local development of market economies – but the people were still the same. Similarly, the close of the Roman period and the onset of the Anglo-Saxon invasions or migrations also witnessed widespread changes in eastern England, but again there was a thread of continuity integrating the landscapes of both Saxon and Viking times. The underlying thread of continuity with the earlier, British, component has not received much archaeological attention to date, although historians have drawn attention to it (Woolf 2003). Paul Everson and David Stocker's paper addresses the problem through the organisation of the landscape. It is a superbly original contribution and I can think of very few archaeological maps (Fig. 1, pg 7) where Bronze Age barrow cemeteries, Iron Age causeways and early monastic foundations are given equal emphasis. And why? Because, to answer the question I posed in the Foreword, they each played a significant role in determining the shape of the landscape in succeeding periods. So what were the cultural links that united them? We don't know at this stage, but I wonder to what extent Bradley's idea of 'ritualisation' could be seen to extend into the post-Roman era? Potentially this could be a very fruitful long-term theme for research - and maybe even a future volume. I have a suspicion that *Time and Tide* could be the start of something remarkable in archaeology: a forum in which specialists of many different periods talk to each other. Let us hope they will find some enlightenment from their different perspectives. Even if eventually they fail, the debate is likely to generate the right sort of heat: it's known as fervour and archaeology cannot thrive without it.

Bibliography

Bradley, R.J., forthcoming, 'In the Dutch mountains: the ritualization of domestic life in Neolithic society' MacDonald lecture, Cambridge University, 2002.

Woolf, A., 2003 'The Britons: from Romans to Barbarians', in Goetz, H-W, Jarnut, J. and Pohl, W. (eds), *Regna and Gentes: the Relationship between Late Antique and Early Medieval Peoples and Kingdoms in the Transformation of the Roman World* (Brill, Leiden), 345-80

INDEX
Page numbers in bold denote Figure references

Abbeys of the Witham valley, 66-74
Agricultural Development Service (ADAS), 58
Agri-environment Schemes, 44, 57, 58
amber beads, 22
Ancient Monuments and Archaeological Areas Act, 1979, 53, 58
Anglesey, 16
Anglian Water, 47
Anglo-Saxon hanging bowl, iv, 28
    sword hilt, 4
    triple brooch, 28, 30
animal bones, 22, 25
anthropoid-hilted dagger, 16
antler, 26
Anwick, 6, 57
Archaeological Project Services, 57
architectural recording, 14
Arts and Humanities Research Board, 41
Augustinian, 66
axe-head, iron, 62, **64**
axe, iron, looped and socketed, 25, **26**

Banks, Sir Joseph, 4, 16, 76
Bardney Abbey, **7**, 11, 55, 66, 67, **68**, 72, 73
Bardney Lock, 16
Bardney, 6, 9, 11, 13, 14, 16, 27, 28, 33, 45, 66, 67
Barleymouth Grange, 11
Barlings, 10, 11, 12, **13**, 14, 27, **55**
    Abbey, 6, **7**, 8, 9, 55, 68, 73
    Eau, 6, 11, 29
    project, 6-12
Barrow-on-Humber, 11
Barton-on-Humber, 11
Battersea Shield, 21
Bede, 6, 11, 67
Benedictine, 11, 66
Bettinson's Bridge, 37, **38**
Bewley, Dr Bob, 50
Bidgood, Councillor Alan, 71
Billingborough, 57
Billinghay, 10, 45
Bog Oaks, 4
bone 'gouges', 21, 26
Bonner, Jim, 43, 81
borehole transects, **34**, 35, **36**
bowls, bronze, 22
Bradley, Richard, 83
Brakespear, Harold, 67
Brandon, Charles, 9
Branston, 28, 30
Branston Fen, 35
Branston Island, 3, 48
Brayford Pool, 3, 6, 33, **34**, 35, **39, 40**, 41
British Academy, 41
British Museum, The, 60
British Sugar, 72
British Trust for Conservation Volunteers, The (BTCV), 70, 71, 72, 73, 74
Bronze Age barrow cemetery, iv, 4, 9, 10, 28, 30, 35, 38, 48, **55**, 83
Bronze Age saltern, 57
Buck, Samuel, 66
Bugthorpe, East Yorkshire, 21
Bullington Priory, **7**, 66, 68
burnt mound, 37
Byng, John, 66

Cadbury, Thomas, 76, 82
Caldicot, South Wales, 29

Campney Grange Farm, **36**, 37
Canterbury Cathedral, 12
Canwick, 48
Car Dyke, 45, 55, 57
carnyx, 4, 16
Catley Priory, 4, **7**, 55, 66, 73
Catney, Steve, 3, 43, 53, 81
Cherry Willingham, 28, 30, 45
Cistercian, 10, 66
City and County Museum, 17, 60, 68, 76-80
claypits, 2
Colchester, 30
Common Agricultural Policy, 44, 58
Community Archaeology, 45
Community Plans, 45
Coningsby, 45, **48**
conservation of excavated finds, 60-65
Conservation Services Team, 44, 49
Countryside and Rights of Way Act, 44
Countryside Commission, 72, 73
Countryside Stewardship Scheme, 43-45, 49, 58, 70, 72, 73
County Environmental Record, 43
Cromwell, Lord, 8, 10
crosses, village and churchyard, 55
cultural resource management, 43-51
currency bar, 26, 30
Curry Report, 44

dagger, iron, 25
    medieval, 12
Danes Graves, 27
de Gant, 9, 67
de la Hayes, 9
de Lacey, 8
de Umfraville, Sir Gilbert, 74
Dean and Chapter of Lincoln Cathedral, 76
dendrochronology, 16, 19, 28, 29, 38, 82
Department for Culture, Media and Sport, 44, 53, 81
Department of Environment, 55
Department of Environment, Food and Rural Affairs (DEFRA), 43, 45, 58, 72
Desription of study area, 3
development control, 43, 45, 46, 49, 52, 53, 81, 82
Dogdyke, 33, 35, 55
drainage, 35
dug-out canoe, see log boat
Durham University, 44

East Fen, 35
East Lindsey District Council, 69, 71, 74
East Lindsey, 3, 45
Eastern bypass, 35, **36**, 37, 45, **46**, 48
ELAES, 44, 45
Electricity Act, 1989, 52
English Heritage, 6, 41, 50, 52, 53, 55, 57, 58, 60, 62, 68, 69, 70, 71, 74, 81, 82
English Rural Development Programme, 58
Environment Act, 1995, 47, 52
Environment Agency, 1, 2, 22, 23, 40, 43, 47-50, 52, 77, 82
environmental analysis, 30
Environmental Impact Assessment Regulations, 47, 52
Environmentally Sensitive Areas, 45, 58
epaulette, **21**, 22
Evans, The Alan, Memorial Trust, 71
Everson, Paul, 6, 55, 76, 83
Exeter University, 52

Fairclough, Graham, 68
Fell, Vanessa, 62
Fengate, 81
Fenland Survey, 37, 52
Fenside Farm, **36**, 37
Field, Naomi, 16, 60, 82
fieldwalking, 14, 50, 73
file, iron, 26, **63**
Finds Liaison Officer, 44
Fiskerton causeway, 16-30
Fiskerton Viking sword, iv, 28, 30
Flag Fen, 20, 27, 29
flood storage, 2, 47
Fossdyke, 33, **39**, 40
Fowler, C.H., 74
Fox, Cyril, 16
French, Charly, 33, 82
Friends of Bardney Abbey, 72
Friends of Tupholme Abbey (FOTA), **70**, 71, 74

Garton Slack, 27
Garton Station, 27
gas pipelines, 35, **46**, 47
General Development Order, 1995, 52
geochemical survey, 30
geographical information system, 43, 50
geography and geology, 3
geophysical survey, 30, 73
Gilbertine, 66
Gipsey Bridge, 37, **38**
Grantham, 3
Greetwell, 47, 48, 49
Greyfriars, 76-79

Hallstatt, B, C, D, 30
Hart's Grounds, 35
Hartsholme, 13
Haskins, Lord, 45
Hatton, 47
Haven, The, 3
Haverholme Priory, **7**, 55, 66
Hayes, Dr Peter, 68
Heighington, 45
Heritage Lincolnshire, 14, 44, 45, 57, 68, 69, 72, 73
Heritage Lottery, 44, 73
Heritage Protection Legislation Reform, 81
Hertford Heath, 21
Historic Landscape Characterisation, 50, 58
Holocene, 33, 37, 40
Horncastle, 16
human bones, 22
Humberside Levels, 52

Icanho, 11
Irchester type, 22
Iron Age coastline, 35
    martial equipment, 21
    metalwork, 16, 26
    pottery, 22
    religion, 16
    spear, **25**
    sword, 16

jet ring, 22
Jews' Court Trust, 14, 72, 73

Kesteven, 3
Kirkburn, 27,
Kirkby on Bain, 47
Kirkstead Abbey, **7**, 55, 66, 73
Kirkstead, 8, 9, 10, 12, 14
Kyme Eau, 3

Kyme Priory, **7**, 66
Kyme, 6, 11, 33, 55, 74
Kysice, Bohemia, 21

La Tène, 16, 19, 21, 27, 29
Laing, Rev Charles, 67, 72
Landfill Tax Rebate Scheme, 72, 73
Latham, Derek and Associates, 70
Leland, John, 11, 67
Leverhulme Trust, 41
Lexden, Essex, 21
LIDAR, 14, 43, 50
Liebau, Germany, 21
limestone rubble, 18, **19**, **23**, 24, 29
linchpins, iron, 22
Lincoln Castle, 9
    City Archaeologist, 45
    Eastern Bypass, 35-37, 45, 46, 48
    Edge, 4
    Gap, 3
    University site, **39, 40**
Lincolnshire Archaeological Handbook, The, 49
Lincolnshire Conservation Services Team, 43
Lincolnshire Rising, 9
Lincolnshire Wildlife Trust, 70
Lindsey, 6, 9,11, 55
linear ditched systems, 48
Linwood Hall Farm, **36**, 37
Llyn Cerrig Bach, 16, 27
log boat, 4, 16, **23**, 24, 25, 60, 65, 76, 77
lunar eclipse, 27, 28, 29, 82

Management of Archaeological Projects (MAP 2), 62-64
Management plan, Tupholme, 69-72
McDonald Institute for Archaeological Research, 41
medieval axe-heads, **10**, 12
    daggers, 12
    pottery, 77
    spearheads, 12
    swords, **10**, 12,
metalworking tools, 21
Metheringham, 45
microware analysis, 21
mineral extraction, **46**, 47, **48**, 49, 52
Ministry of Agriculture, Fisheries and Food (MAFF), 72
moated sites, 55
Monaghan, J. M., 37
Monks Abbey, **7**, 11, 12
Monument Trust, the, 71
Monuments At Risk in England's Wetlands Project (MAREW), 52, 58
Monuments At Risk Survey (MARS), 52, 58
Monuments Protection Programme (MPP), 53, 55, **56**, 57, 58, 81
Museum Association, The, 76

National Historical Building Crafts Institute, 70
National Mapping Programme, 13, 14
National Trust, The, 14
Nene Valley Research Committee, 81
Neolithic axes, 28, 30
    long barrow, 4
Nettleham, Bishop's Palace, 55
Nocton Delph, 3
    Fen, 35
    Priory, **7**, 66, 68
North Kesteven Medieval Trail, 73, 74
North Kesteven, 45, 73, 74
North Lincolnshire Archaeological Unit, 17
notched planks, 18
Nottingham University, 73

Omex Agricultural Ltd, 72, 73
organic residue analysis, 64
Oxney, 6

Palaeochannels, 4, 40, 41
Palaeoenvironmental research, 33-42, 82
Palaeolithic hand axe, 4, 30
Panter, Ian, 60, 62
Panter-Hudspith, 78
Parker Pearson, Mike, 16, 82
Peach, Alison, 53
Pearson, Dr George, 76
peg holes, 18
Pelham's Lands, 35
Peterborough Abbey, 11, 28, 46
photogrammetric survey, 70
Planning Policy Guidance Note 15, 46
Planning Policy Guidance Note 16, 43, 46, 47, 52, 64
Potterhanworth, 4
pottery analysis, 14
    medieval, 77
Pre-Construct Archaeology, 22, 50, 60
Premonstratensian, 6, 66
Pryor, Frances, iv, 81

Quaternary, 4
Queen Elizabeth Grammar School, Horncastle, 70

Rackham, James, 33, 82
radiocarbon dates, **38, 40**
reaping hook, iron, 22
Revesby, 55
Riseholme Agricultural College, 70
ritualisation, 83
River Bain, 3, 6, 33, 45, **48**
    Slea, 6, 33, 35
    Thames, 16, 27, 28
    Till, 33, 39
Robson, J.D., 35, 37
Roman barrows, 55
    coastline, 35
    'hard', 46
    metalwork, 16
    pottery, 22, 23
    sanctuaries, 28, 30
    settlement, 28
Romano-British settlement, 48
Roughton, 55
roundel, bronze 21
Royal Air Force College, Cranwell, 71
Royal Commission on the Historical Monuments of England
    (RCHME), 68, 70, 73
Rural Action Zone, 50
Rural Development Commission, 73
Rural Development Regulation (Agenda 2000), 58
Rural White Paper, 44
Rylatt, Jim, 16, 82

SAROS cycle, 28, 29
saw, iron, 22, **61**
scabbard, iron, 21
scabbard, wooden, **61**
scheduled monuments, 53, **54, 56**, 57, 68
Seney Place, 55
Sheffield University, 82
Short Ferry, 16, 35, 60
Sibsey windmill, 55
Silk Willoughby, 47
sites and monument record, 4, 43, 44, 49, 50, 53
Skertchly, S.B.J.,35
Soay sheep, 70
Society of Museum Archaeologists, The, 64

Somerset Levels, 52
South Holland, 50
South Whitham, 3
Southrey, **36**, 37, 45, 55
spearheads, iron, 21
    medieval, 12
S-shaped bronze article, **21**, 22, 27
St. Andrew's Church, Bardney, **11**
St. Leonard's Chapel, Kirkstead, 12, 73
St. Mary and All Saints Church, Kyme, 74
St. Oswald, 6, 8, 11, 67
Stainfield Nunnery, 7, 11, 14, 55, 66
Stainfield, 38, **55**, 68
Stamp End, 6, 11, 16
Stark, Adam, 76
Start, David, 66, 81, 82
Stixwould burnt mound, 37, **38**
Stixwould Priory, 7, 12, 14, 55, 66
Stocker, David, 6, 53, 55, 67, 76, 83
Stuffins, Vernon, 16, 82
Stukeley, William, **66**
Swan Pool, 33, **34**
sword handle, bronze, 21
sword, medieval, **10**, 12

Tattershall Thorpe defended enclosure, 55
Tattershall, 3, 6, 8-12, 14, 16, 27, 33, **38**, 45, 47, **48**
The Wash, 3
topographical survey, 14, 50
town and country planning legislation, 45, 52
Transco, 47
Tumby, 47
Tupholme Abbey, **7**, 11, 14, 55, 66, 68-72, **69-71**

Urban Archaeological Database, 13, 43
Usborne, Andrew, 1, 82

Vale, David, 71
Viking sword, iv, 28, 30
Viking Way, 71
village and churchyard crosses, 55

Walcott, 55, 57
Walcott Common, 37, **38**
Walcott longbarrow, 55
Washingborough Archaeology Group, 30
Washingborough, iv, 3, 11, 16, 27, 28, 29, 30, 37, **38**, 45, 48
Water Industry Act, 1991, 52
Went, Dave, 52, 81
West Fen, 33, 35
West Lindsey District Council, 72, 73, 74
West Lindsey, 45, 68
wetland reserve, 2
Wetwang Slack, 21, 27
Wheeler, 35
White, Andrew, 67
White, Rob, 60, 82
Witham scabbard, 16
Witham Shield, iv, 4, 16, 60
Witham Valley Archaeology Research Committee, iv, 3, 5, 81, 82
Wildmoor Fen, 33, 35
Wise, Julia, 53
Wolds Interpretation Strategy, 49
Woodhall Spa, 35, 37, **38**, 45, 57
woodworking tools, 21,
Wright, The J.W., Trust,73

X-radiography, 62, **63, 64**
X-ray fluorescence spectrometry, 64

York, 11